Name caleb

4X4
OffRoad

GMC

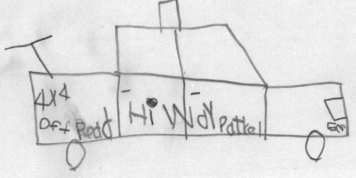

4X4
Off Road
Hi Widy Patrel
GMC

I Can Draw...
Cars & Trucks

Artwork by Terry Longhurst

Text by Amanda O'Neill

p

This is a Parragon Publishing Book
This edition published in 2005

Parragon Publishing
Queen Street House
4 Queen Street
Bath BA1 1HE, UK

Designed, packaged, and produced by
Touchstone

ISBN 1-40545-772-4

Artwork by Terry Longhurst
Text by Amanda O'Neill
Edited by Philip de Ste. Croix

Printed in China

About this book

Everybody can enjoy drawing, but sometimes it's hard to know where to begin. The subject you want to draw can look very complicated. This book shows you how to start, by breaking down your subject into a series of simple shapes.

The tools you need are very simple. The basic requirements are paper and pencils. Very thin paper wears through if you have to rub out a line, so choose paper that is thick enough to work on. Pencils come with different leads, from very hard to very soft. Very hard pencils give a clean, thin line which is best for finishing drawings. Very soft ones give a thicker, darker line. You will probably find a medium pencil most useful.

If you want to color in your drawing, you have the choice of paints, colored inks, or felt-tip pens. Fine felt-tips are useful for drawing outlines, thick felt-tips are better for coloring in.

The most important tool you have is your own eyes. The mistake many people make is to draw what they think something looks like, instead of really looking at it carefully first. Half the secret of making your drawing look good is getting the proportions right. Study your subject before you start, and break it down in your mind into sections. Check how much bigger, or longer, or shorter, one part is than another. Notice where one part joins another, and at what angle. See where there are flowing curves, and where there are straight lines.

The step-by-step drawings in this book show you exactly how to do this. Each subject is broken down into easy stages, so you can build up your drawing one piece at a time. Look carefully at each shape before – and after – you draw it. If you find you have drawn it the wrong size or in the wrong place, correct it before you go on. Then the next shape will fit into place, and piece-by-piece you can build up a fantastic picture.

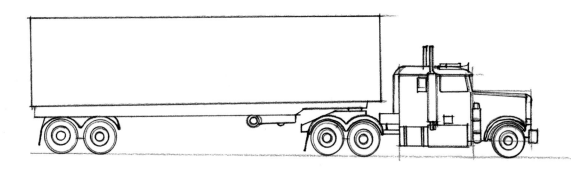

Ferrari F50

Be careful to get these first shapes right.

Supercars like this are more like racers than ordinary passenger vehicles. This F50 is built with the same care as Ferrari's famous racing cars, with sleek, aggressive lines and a powerful engine.

Start to build up the front of the car. The powerful hood takes up much of the drawing.

Draw in arched shapes for the wheels.

This is a long, low car, so be careful not to make the roof too high.

Now add the spoiler on the back of the car.

Smooth, flowing curves reduce air resistance and increase speed.

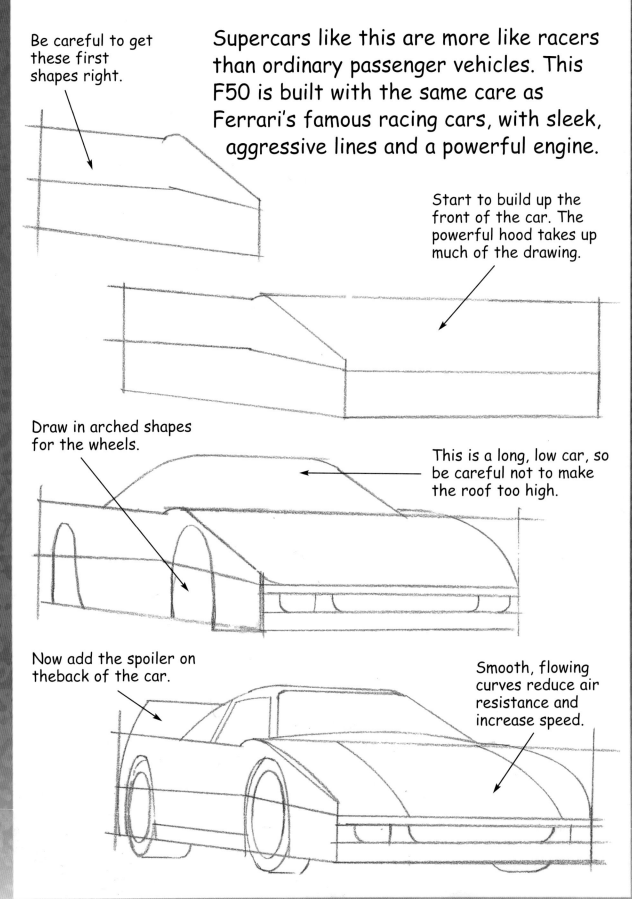

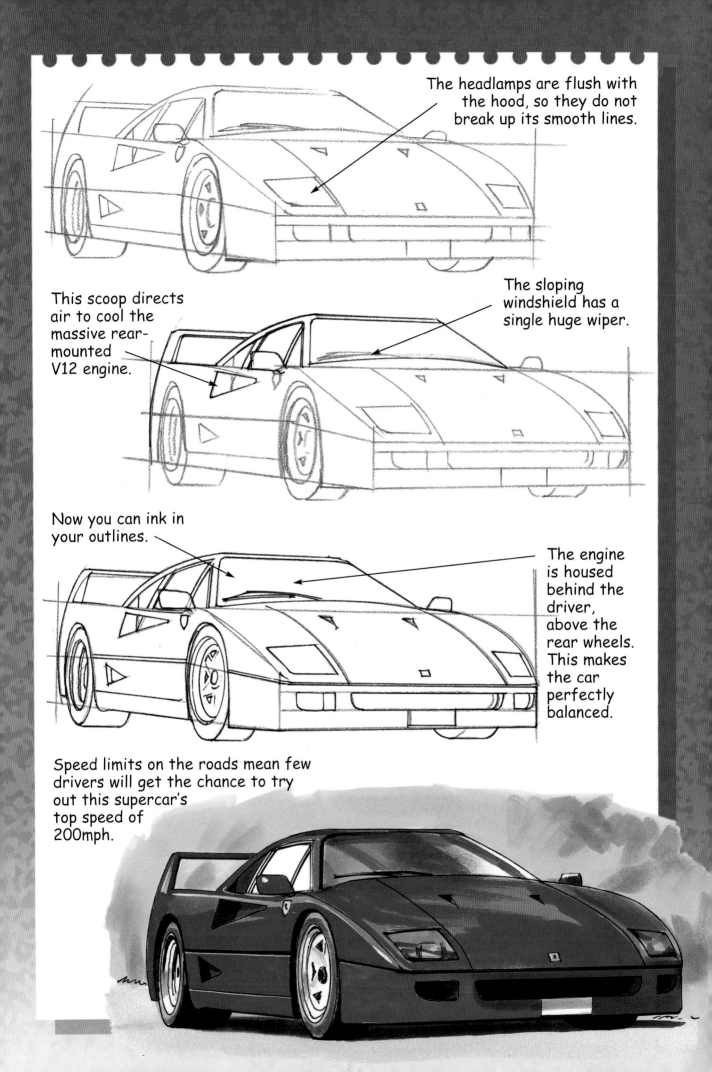

The headlamps are flush with the hood, so they do not break up its smooth lines.

This scoop directs air to cool the massive rear-mounted V12 engine.

The sloping windshield has a single huge wiper.

Now you can ink in your outlines.

The engine is housed behind the driver, above the rear wheels. This makes the car perfectly balanced.

Speed limits on the roads mean few drivers will get the chance to try out this supercar's top speed of 200mph.

Excavator

A familiar vehicle on construction sites, the earthmover clears the ground of rubble and moves vast quantities of soil to enable foundation work to begin. A skilled operator sits in the central cab which pivots full circle on the sturdy 'caterpillar' tracks.

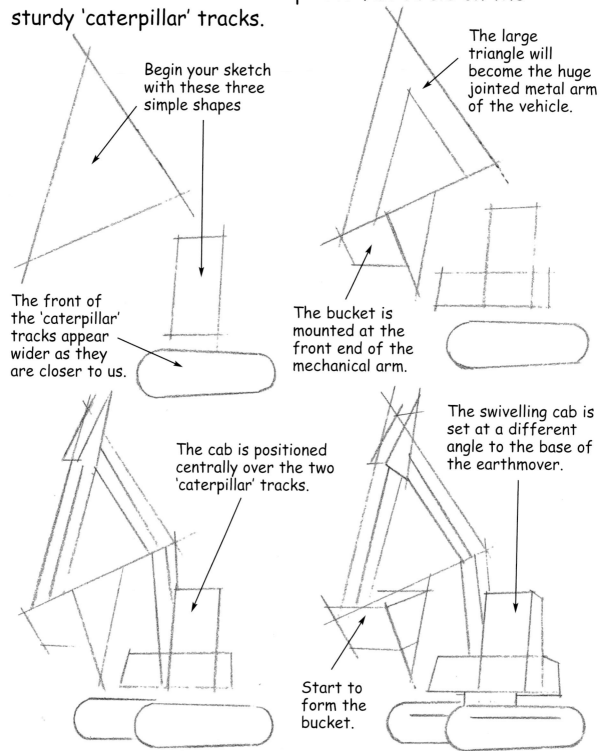

Begin your sketch with these three simple shapes

The large triangle will become the huge jointed metal arm of the vehicle.

The front of the 'caterpillar' tracks appear wider as they are closer to us.

The bucket is mounted at the front end of the mechanical arm.

The cab is positioned centrally over the two 'caterpillar' tracks.

The swivelling cab is set at a different angle to the base of the earthmover.

Start to form the bucket.

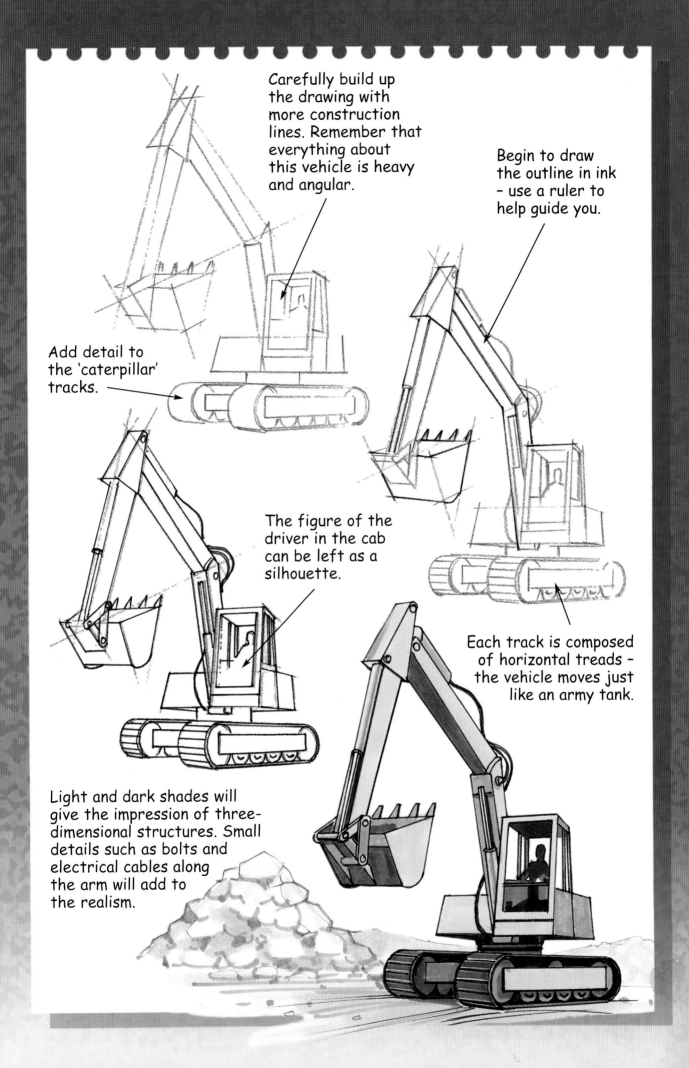

Carefully build up the drawing with more construction lines. Remember that everything about this vehicle is heavy and angular.

Begin to draw the outline in ink – use a ruler to help guide you.

Add detail to the 'caterpillar' tracks.

The figure of the driver in the cab can be left as a silhouette.

Each track is composed of horizontal treads – the vehicle moves just like an army tank.

Light and dark shades will give the impression of three-dimensional structures. Small details such as bolts and electrical cables along the arm will add to the realism.

Mini Cooper

Introduced in 1961, this is the rally version of the famous Mini. Rally cars, designed for racing on public roads, may look very similar to standard models – but they are much faster, with more powerful engines.

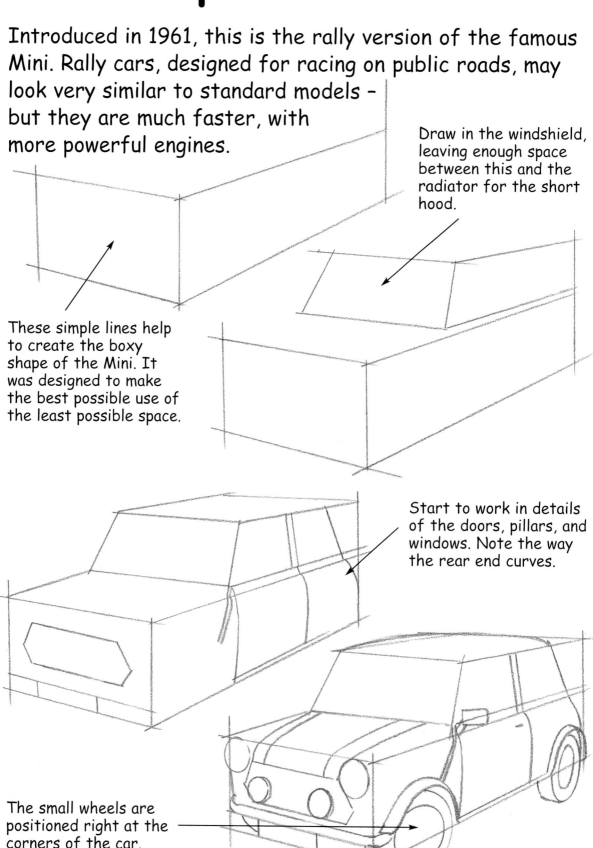

Draw in the windshield, leaving enough space between this and the radiator for the short hood.

These simple lines help to create the boxy shape of the Mini. It was designed to make the best possible use of the least possible space.

Start to work in details of the doors, pillars, and windows. Note the way the rear end curves.

The small wheels are positioned right at the corners of the car.

Now you can start filling in the details, from radiator grille to sun roof. Don't forget those serious lamps on the front!

Light reflecting off the windshield cuts down our view inside, so only part of the interior is visible.

The white stripes on the hood distinguish the Cooper from other Mini models.

In 1964, 1965, and 1967 a Mini Cooper raced to victory in the famous Monte Carlo Rally. A few years later the company stopped making this model – but it was revived in 1990.

With a top speed of 85mph, the Mini Cooper is 15mph faster than the standard Mini.

Mercedes-Benz Truck

Trucks carry nearly all the goods and materials we use. They are big, heavy vehicles, but modern trucks like this are still as streamlined as possible.

At the top is the air deflector. It directs the airstream over the vehicle, so improving the aerodynamics of the truck.

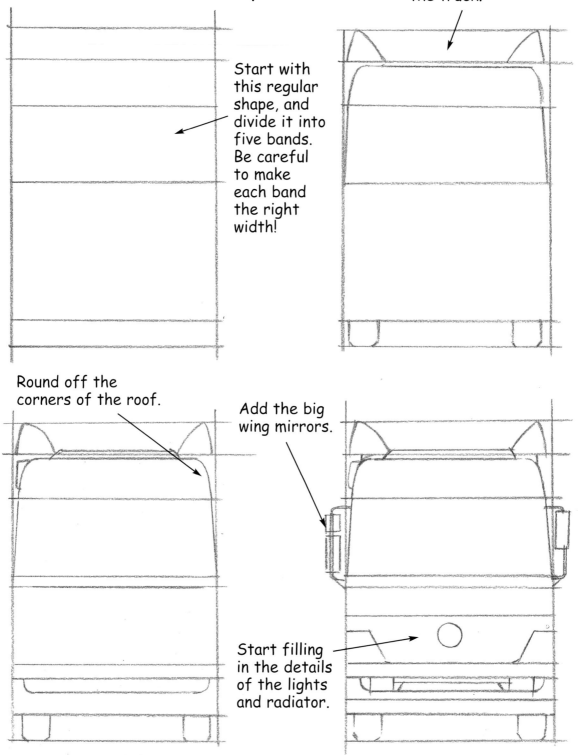

Start with this regular shape, and divide it into five bands. Be careful to make each band the right width!

Round off the corners of the roof.

Add the big wing mirrors.

Start filling in the details of the lights and radiator.

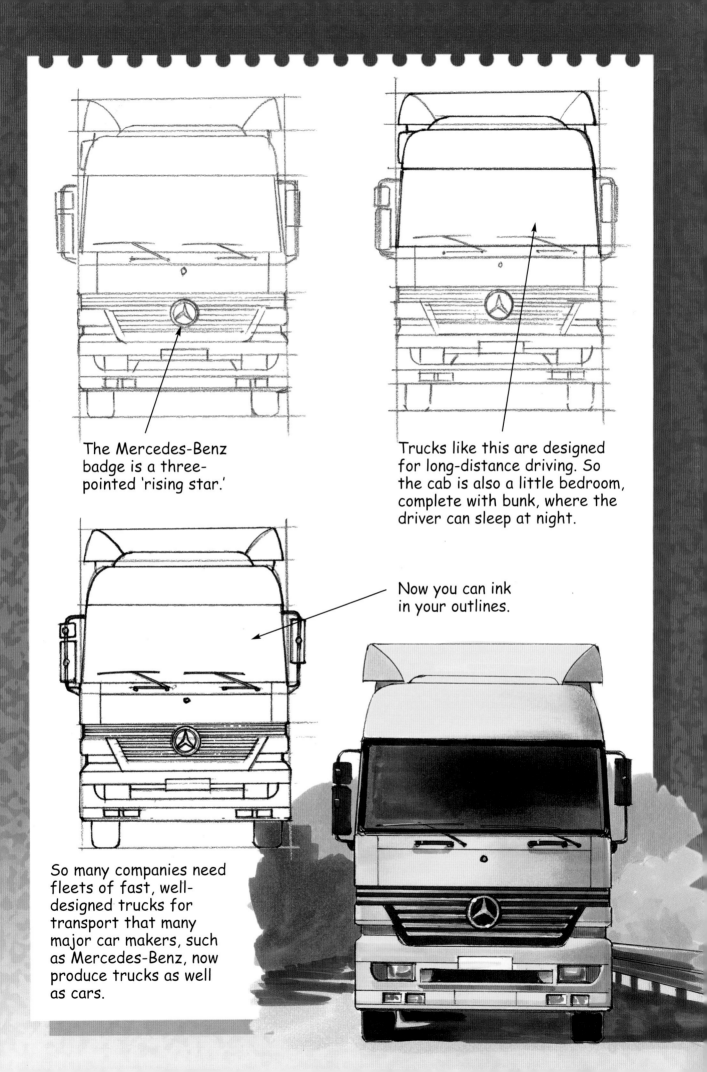

The Mercedes-Benz badge is a three-pointed 'rising star.'

Trucks like this are designed for long-distance driving. So the cab is also a little bedroom, complete with bunk, where the driver can sleep at night.

Now you can ink in your outlines.

So many companies need fleets of fast, well-designed trucks for transport that many major car makers, such as Mercedes-Benz, now produce trucks as well as cars.

Cadillac Coupe de Ville

Big luxury cars like this were very popular in the 1950s. Made for maximum comfort in long-distance travel along America's highways, they looked wonderful, but used incredible amounts of fuel. When gas became more expensive, they went out of fashion.

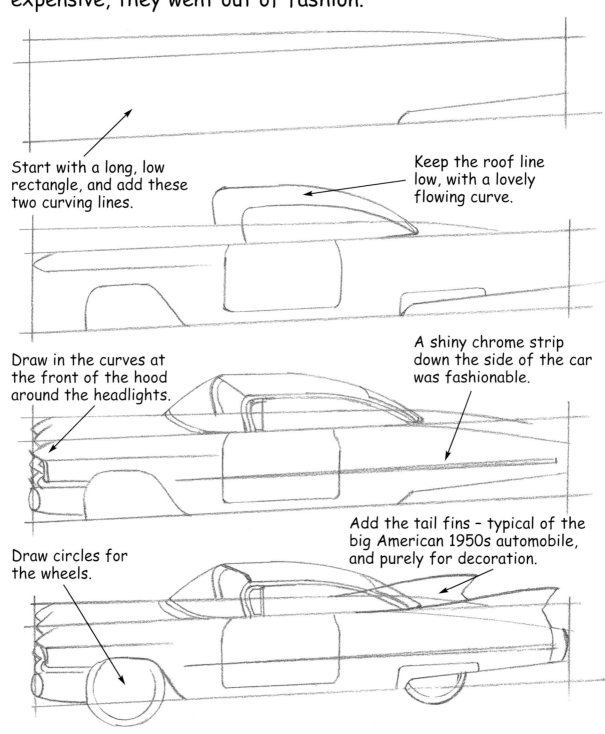

Start with a long, low rectangle, and add these two curving lines.

Keep the roof line low, with a lovely flowing curve.

Draw in the curves at the front of the hood around the headlights.

A shiny chrome strip down the side of the car was fashionable.

Add the tail fins – typical of the big American 1950s automobile, and purely for decoration.

Draw circles for the wheels.

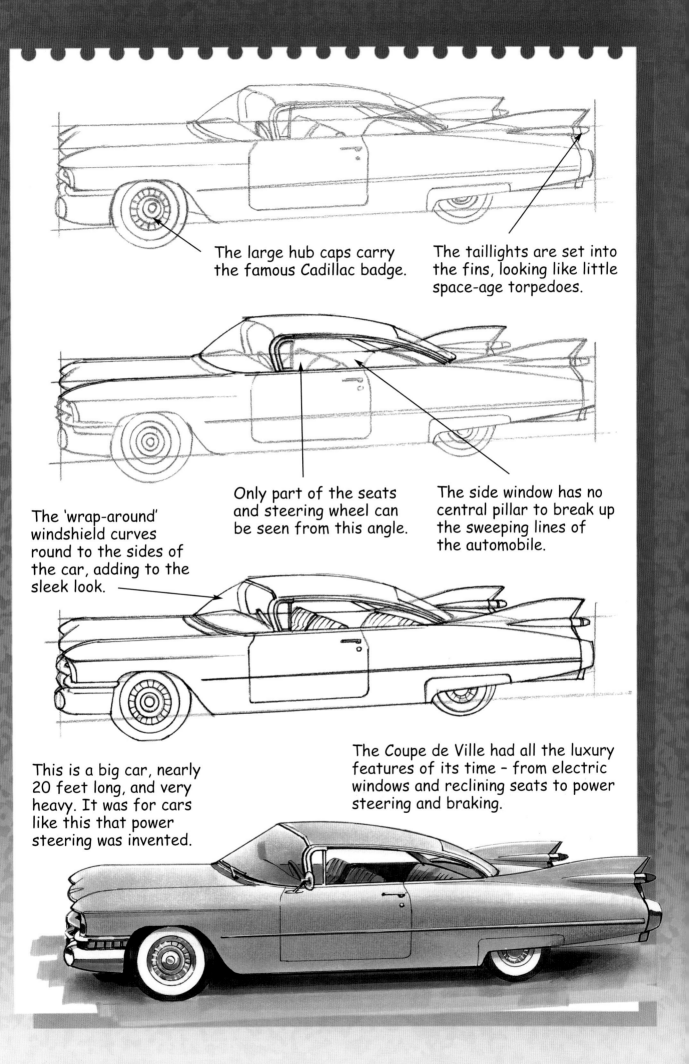

The large hub caps carry the famous Cadillac badge.

The taillights are set into the fins, looking like little space-age torpedoes.

The 'wrap-around' windshield curves round to the sides of the car, adding to the sleek look.

Only part of the seats and steering wheel can be seen from this angle.

The side window has no central pillar to break up the sweeping lines of the automobile.

This is a big car, nearly 20 feet long, and very heavy. It was for cars like this that power steering was invented.

The Coupe de Ville had all the luxury features of its time – from electric windows and reclining seats to power steering and braking.

Transporter

This type of truck consists of two parts. The front part is a 'tractor unit' containing the engine and driver's cab. The back part is a flatbed trailer to carry the load. They are attached by an articulated joint. Different types of load can be fitted on to the flat base of the trailer.

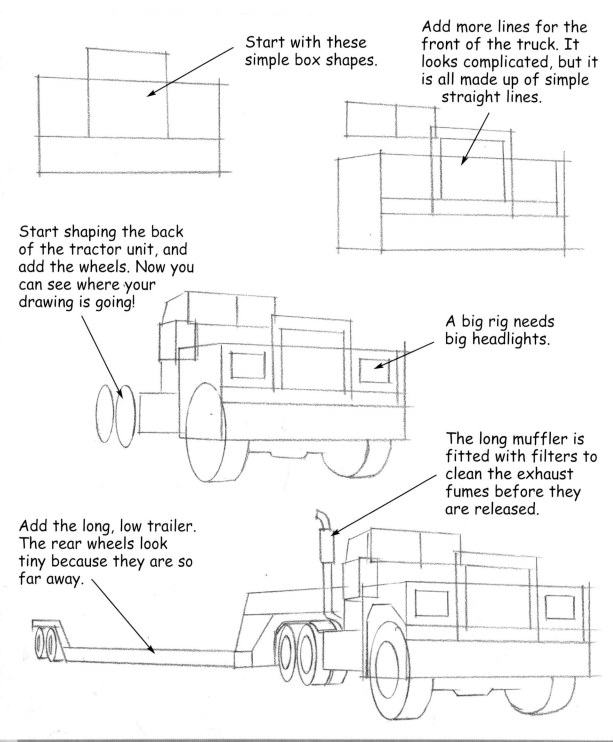

Start with these simple box shapes.

Add more lines for the front of the truck. It looks complicated, but it is all made up of simple straight lines.

Start shaping the back of the tractor unit, and add the wheels. Now you can see where your drawing is going!

A big rig needs big headlights.

The long muffler is fitted with filters to clean the exhaust fumes before they are released.

Add the long, low trailer. The rear wheels look tiny because they are so far away.

Various kinds of trailer can be fitted to the tractor unit. This is a low-loader, built very close to the ground, which is used to carry heavy loads.

Curve the corners of the radiator grille.

Giant rigs like this drive long distances, so the driver's cab is built for comfort – and safety. .

The axle between the rear wheels of the tractor unit carries the massive weight of both the truck and its load.

Finish inking in your outline.

From this angle, this impressive transporter looks every inch the giant it is. It can carry loads that nothing else on the road can handle.

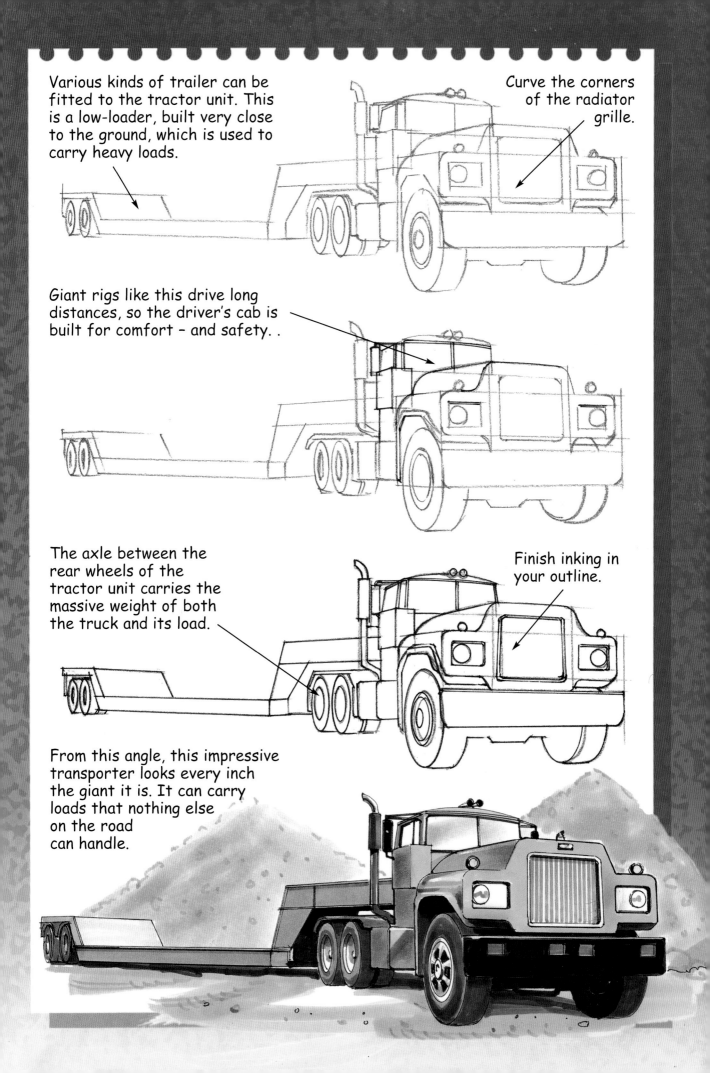

Waste Disposal Truck

This truck collects garbage from homes and takes it to a disposal site to be burned, dumped, or recycled. The garbage is loaded into a hopper at the back, where it is mechanically crushed. Squashed to a quarter of its original size, it is stored in the main body of the truck.

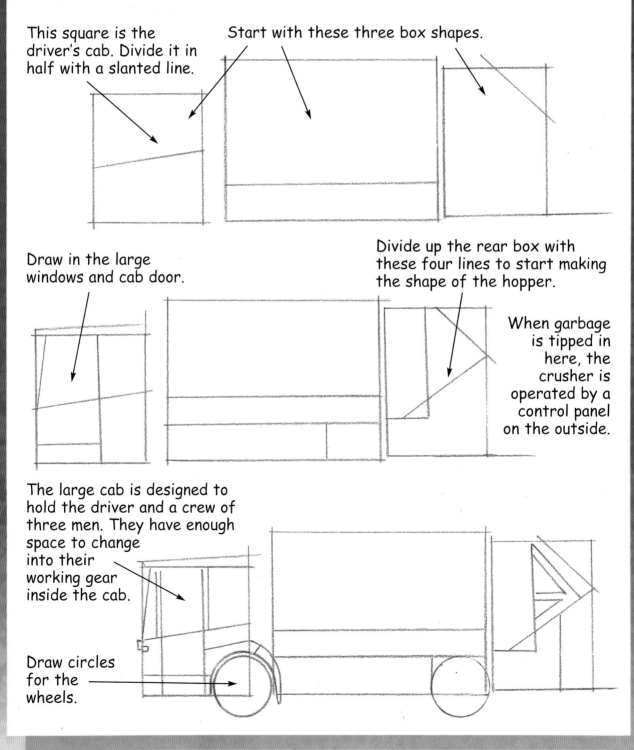

This square is the driver's cab. Divide it in half with a slanted line.

Start with these three box shapes.

Draw in the large windows and cab door.

Divide up the rear box with these four lines to start making the shape of the hopper.

When garbage is tipped in here, the crusher is operated by a control panel on the outside.

The large cab is designed to hold the driver and a crew of three men. They have enough space to change into their working gear inside the cab.

Draw circles for the wheels.

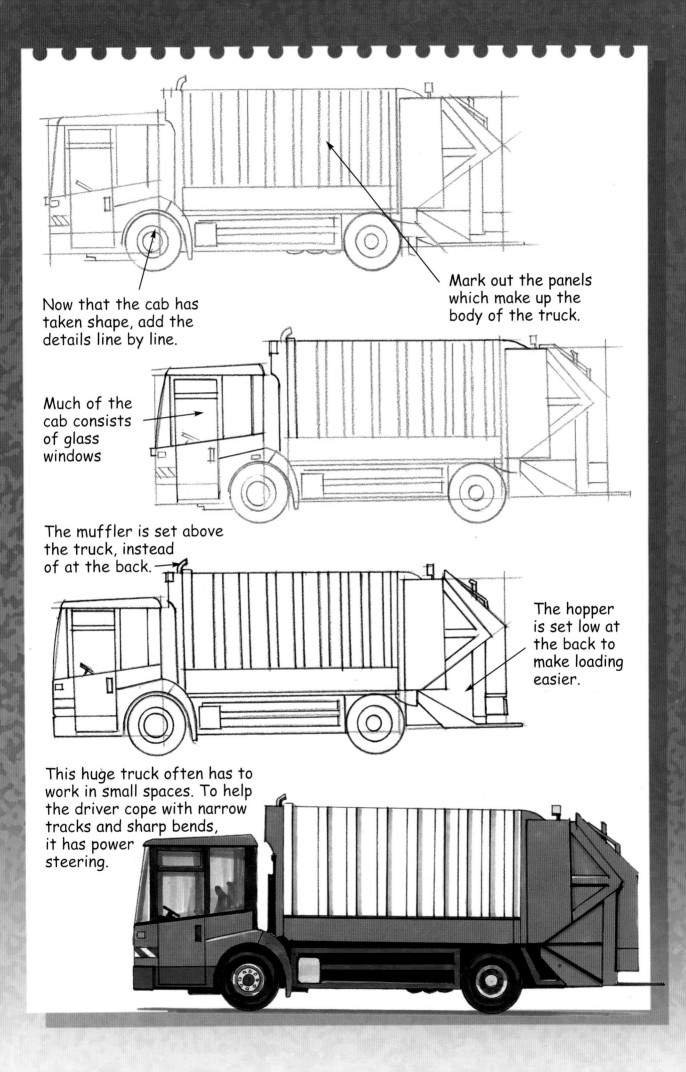

Now that the cab has taken shape, add the details line by line.

Mark out the panels which make up the body of the truck.

Much of the cab consists of glass windows

The muffler is set above the truck, instead of at the back.

The hopper is set low at the back to make loading easier.

This huge truck often has to work in small spaces. To help the driver cope with narrow tracks and sharp bends, it has power steering.

Digger

Tractors can be fitted out with all kinds of machinery for different jobs. They may carry a broad shovel-like blade, for a bulldozer, or a scoop, like this digger. The digger is used to excavate and clear piles of earth and rubble. You will see it on building sites and at road works.

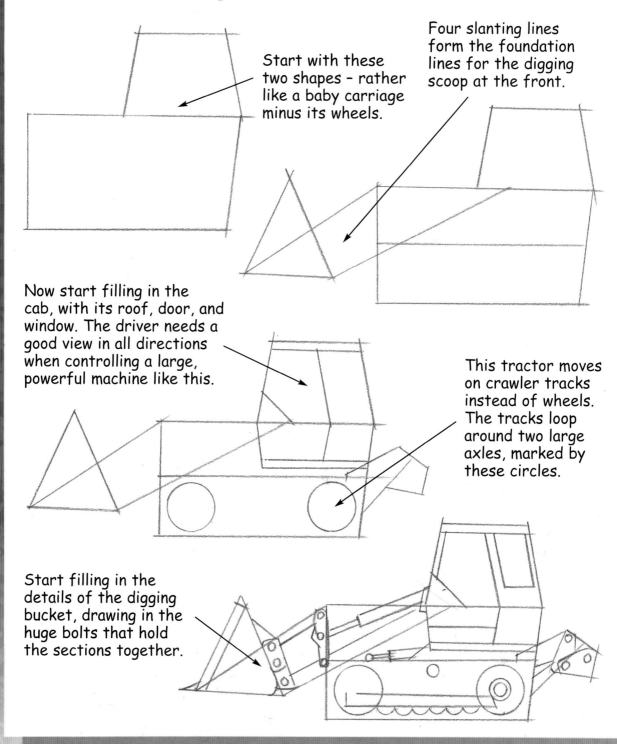

Start with these two shapes – rather like a baby carriage minus its wheels.

Four slanting lines form the foundation lines for the digging scoop at the front.

Now start filling in the cab, with its roof, door, and window. The driver needs a good view in all directions when controlling a large, powerful machine like this.

This tractor moves on crawler tracks instead of wheels. The tracks loop around two large axles, marked by these circles.

Start filling in the details of the digging bucket, drawing in the huge bolts that hold the sections together.

The driver can raise and lower the scoop using controls in his cab.

The back is fitted with giant 'claws,' used to help flatten and spread the scoop's load when it is tipped out.

Link the two big wheels with a system of rods and a chain – like a giant bicycle chain. A motor turns the driving roller that powers the chain.

The 'arms' that move the scoop are activated by hydraulic rams, which provide the power needed.

Now you can draw in the caterpillar track – a huge, flexible belt that allows the tractor to move easily over bumpy ground.

Crawler tractors are ideal where ground is soft or uneven. The tracks help to spread the weight of the vehicle evenly and stop the soil getting compacted.

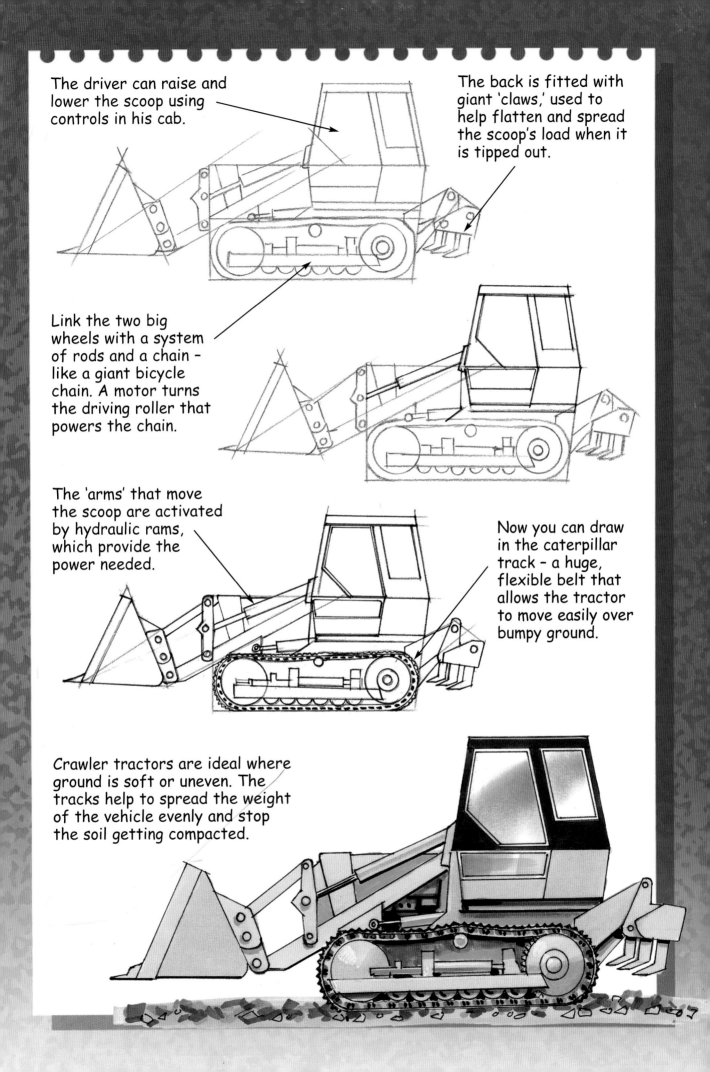

Land Rover Defender

The Land Rover first appeared in 1948 as a tough 'work-horse' based on the army jeep. Made for rough ground, heavy loads and needing little maintenance, it proved ideal for farmers and the military. Later models include luxury versions like the Discovery and Range Rover.

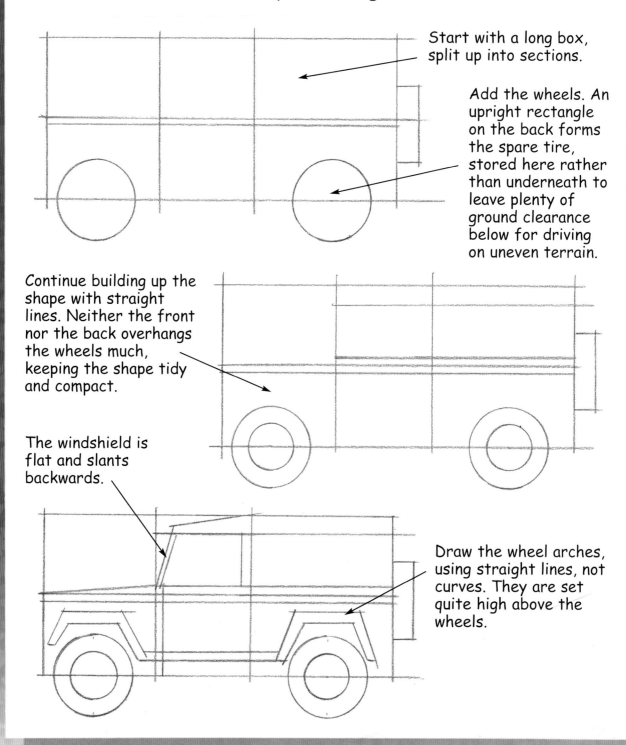

Start with a long box, split up into sections.

Add the wheels. An upright rectangle on the back forms the spare tire, stored here rather than underneath to leave plenty of ground clearance below for driving on uneven terrain.

Continue building up the shape with straight lines. Neither the front nor the back overhangs the wheels much, keeping the shape tidy and compact.

The windshield is flat and slants backwards.

Draw the wheel arches, using straight lines, not curves. They are set quite high above the wheels.

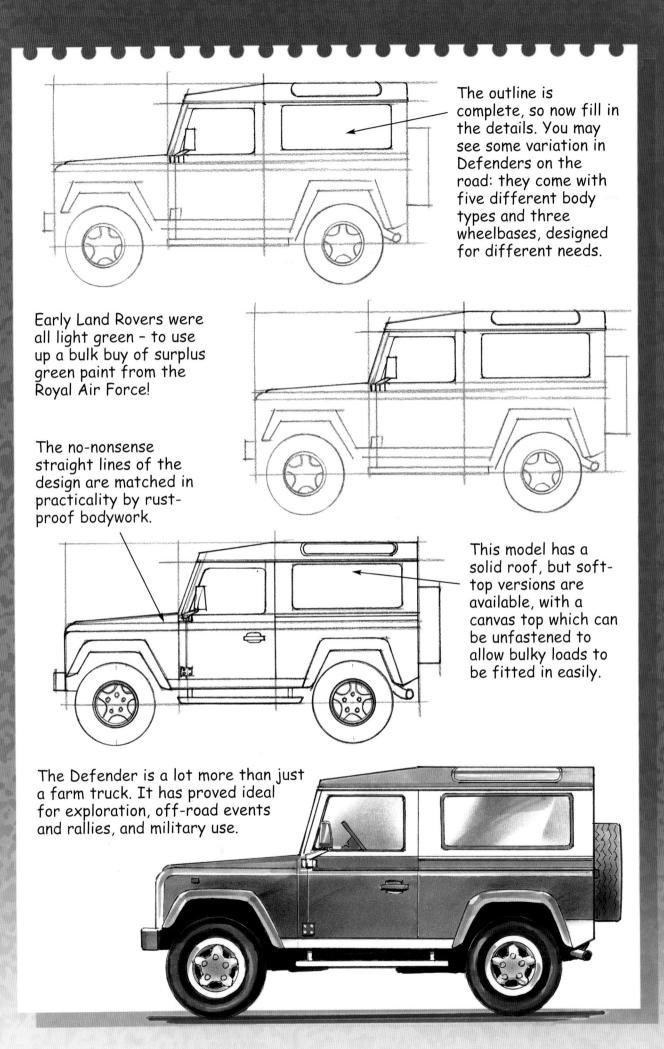

The outline is complete, so now fill in the details. You may see some variation in Defenders on the road: they come with five different body types and three wheelbases, designed for different needs.

Early Land Rovers were all light green – to use up a bulk buy of surplus green paint from the Royal Air Force!

The no-nonsense straight lines of the design are matched in practicality by rust-proof bodywork.

This model has a solid roof, but soft-top versions are available, with a canvas top which can be unfastened to allow bulky loads to be fitted in easily.

The Defender is a lot more than just a farm truck. It has proved ideal for exploration, off-road events and rallies, and military use.

Forklift Truck

This is a handy little work-horse used to transport heavy loads short distances on site. It can carry bricks on a building site, or move pallets from a delivery lorry into a warehouse. It is small enough to carry its load into a building and deliver it directly to the storage bays.

These three simple shapes form the main part of this little vehicle.

The engine is positioned at the rear, so the body sticks out behind.

This upright piece stops the load tipping backward on to the driver.

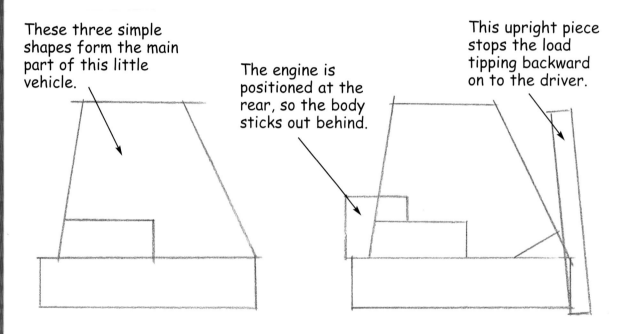

Draw in a simple seat and start on the driver. An oblong and a circle don't look much like a human being – yet. But soon they will!

This long tube is the muffler, placed here to direct fumes away from the driver.

Add arms and legs, curve the shoulders, and suddenly we have quite a convincing driver. The shape in front of him houses the steering column, with the steering wheel under his hands.

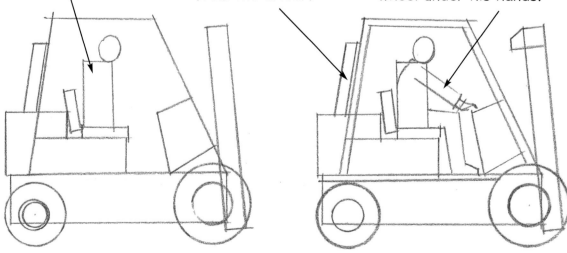

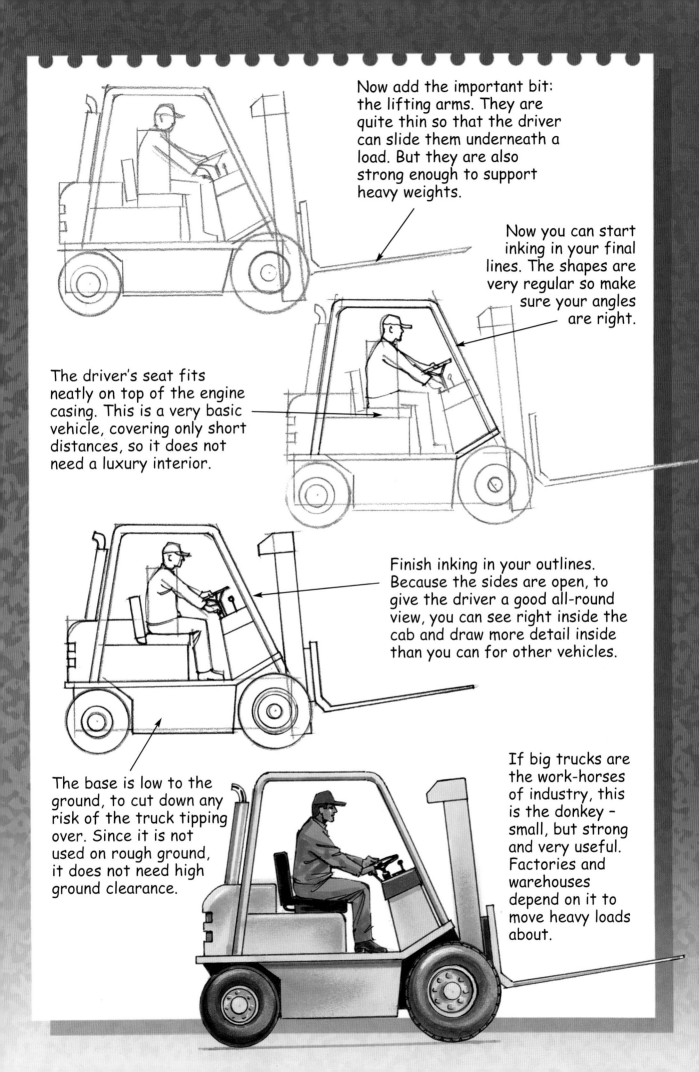

Now add the important bit: the lifting arms. They are quite thin so that the driver can slide them underneath a load. But they are also strong enough to support heavy weights.

Now you can start inking in your final lines. The shapes are very regular so make sure your angles are right.

The driver's seat fits neatly on top of the engine casing. This is a very basic vehicle, covering only short distances, so it does not need a luxury interior.

Finish inking in your outlines. Because the sides are open, to give the driver a good all-round view, you can see right inside the cab and draw more detail inside than you can for other vehicles.

The base is low to the ground, to cut down any risk of the truck tipping over. Since it is not used on rough ground, it does not need high ground clearance.

If big trucks are the work-horses of industry, this is the donkey – small, but strong and very useful. Factories and warehouses depend on it to move heavy loads about.

Tractor

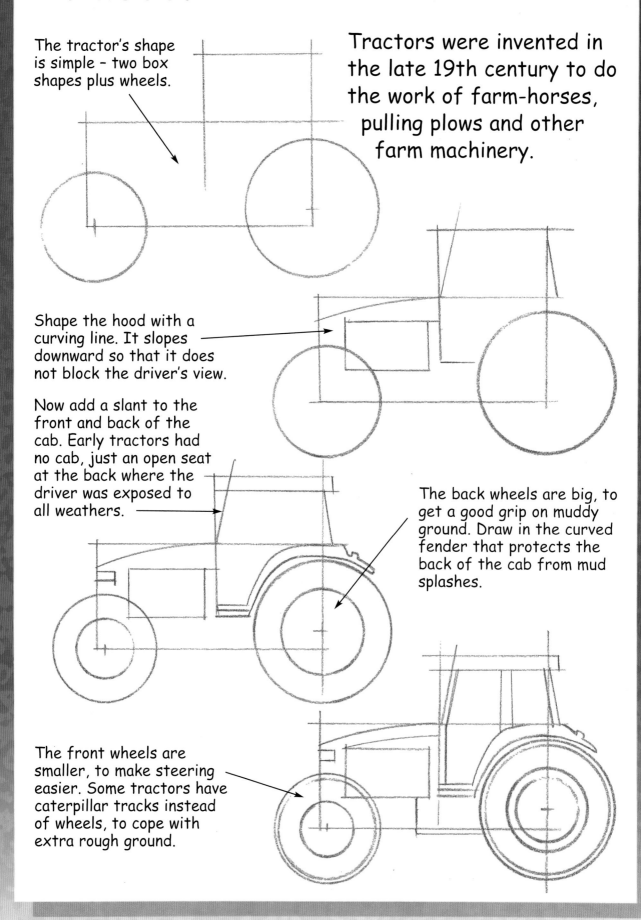

The tractor's shape is simple – two box shapes plus wheels.

Tractors were invented in the late 19th century to do the work of farm-horses, pulling plows and other farm machinery.

Shape the hood with a curving line. It slopes downward so that it does not block the driver's view.

Now add a slant to the front and back of the cab. Early tractors had no cab, just an open seat at the back where the driver was exposed to all weathers.

The back wheels are big, to get a good grip on muddy ground. Draw in the curved fender that protects the back of the cab from mud splashes.

The front wheels are smaller, to make steering easier. Some tractors have caterpillar tracks instead of wheels, to cope with extra rough ground.

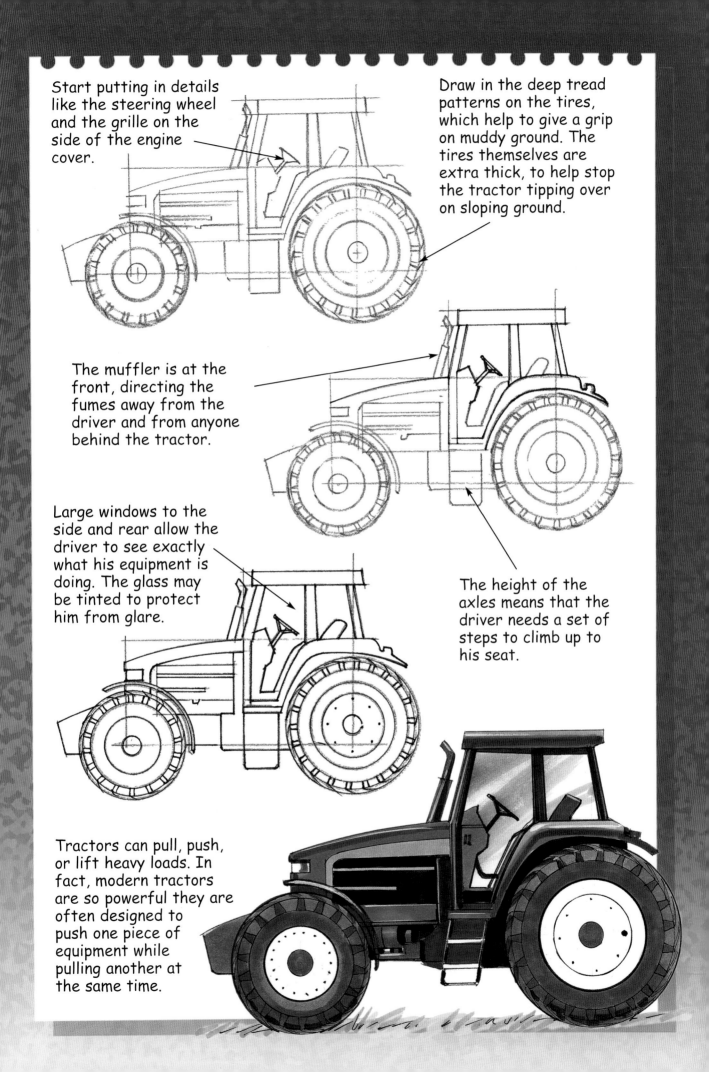

Start putting in details like the steering wheel and the grille on the side of the engine cover.

Draw in the deep tread patterns on the tires, which help to give a grip on muddy ground. The tires themselves are extra thick, to help stop the tractor tipping over on sloping ground.

The muffler is at the front, directing the fumes away from the driver and from anyone behind the tractor.

Large windows to the side and rear allow the driver to see exactly what his equipment is doing. The glass may be tinted to protect him from glare.

The height of the axles means that the driver needs a set of steps to climb up to his seat.

Tractors can pull, push, or lift heavy loads. In fact, modern tractors are so powerful they are often designed to push one piece of equipment while pulling another at the same time.

Jaguar XJS

Most cars are designed in a practical way, for reliability, space, comfort, and fuel economy. Sports cars like this Jaguar are designed for enjoyment. They put speed, power, and good looks first. The XJS first appeared in 1975. It had a big V12 engine and could reach 150mph.

Start with a long box. Divide it into three uneven layers, then mark out the lines of the windows and the position of the wheel arches.

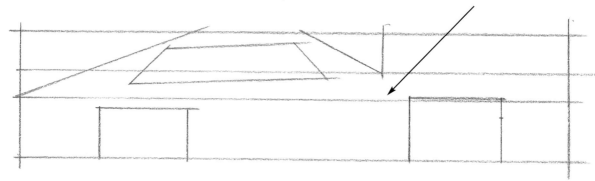

Now fit the wheels into the spaces marked out for them.

Early Jaguars, like many such sports cars, were open two-seaters. Today, often sports cars are closed four-seater coupés like this.

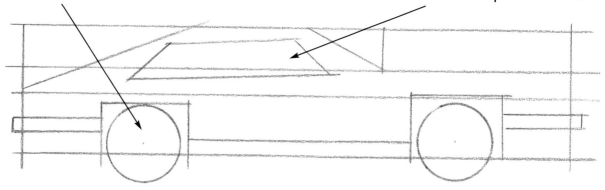

Start filling in details like the central pillar of the window, and the door.

Now start shaping the front of the hood. The top and underside taper gently toward the front. Now you can see the sleek lines of the automobile.

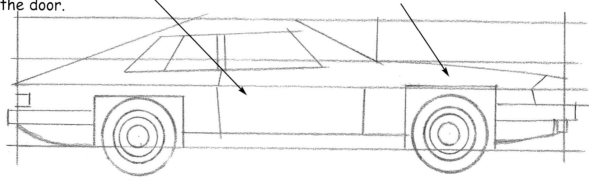

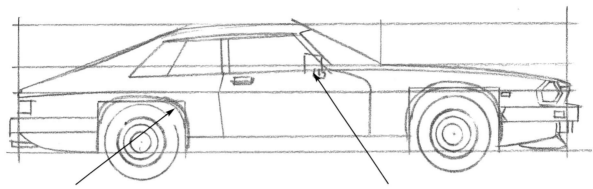

Draw in the wheel
arches, which flare out
slightly from the body.

Now you can add the smaller details – the door
handle, wing mirror, and head- and tail-lights.
Note the unusual shape of the headlights.

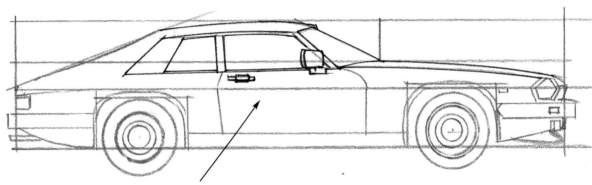

This is a luxury car, with a smooth, powerful engine
and electronic seats. It is just as finely finished
inside, with hand-sewn leather seats.

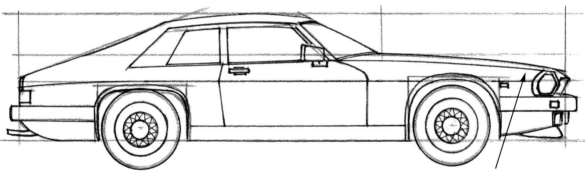

For safety reasons, Jaguars no
longer bear the famous 'big cat'
mascot on the hood, which might
cause injuries in an accident.

The powerful engine
means this car can reach
a speed of 100mph in
just 16 seconds.

American Truck

Huge articulated trucks travel America's freeways. These 'big rigs' are part of the American legend, and, along with their drivers, are the heroes of many road movies.

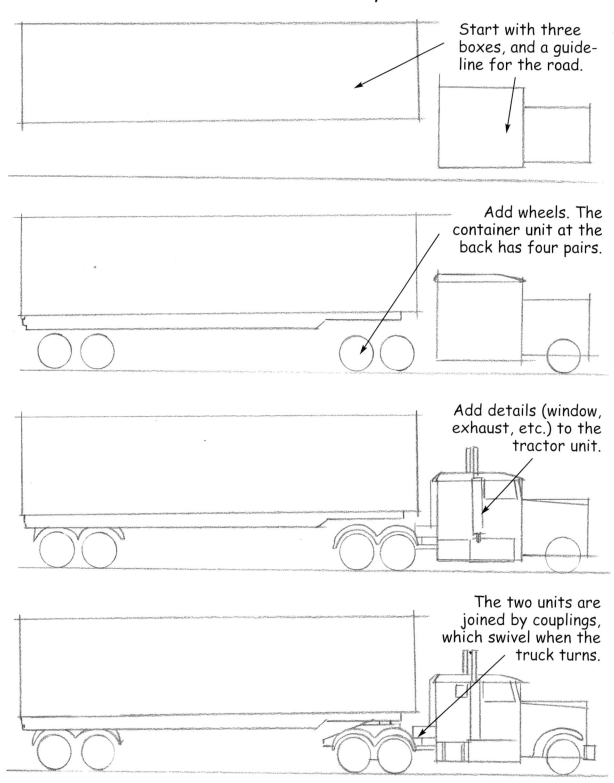

Start with three boxes, and a guide-line for the road.

Add wheels. The container unit at the back has four pairs.

Add details (window, exhaust, etc.) to the tractor unit.

The two units are joined by couplings, which swivel when the truck turns.

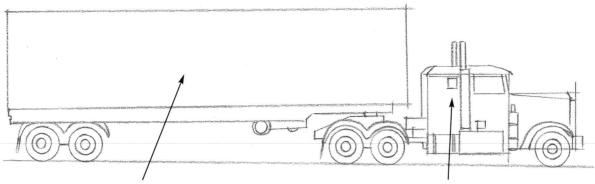

Container units, known as semi-trailers, vary in shape. Different kinds are designed to carry liquids, food, refrigerated goods, etc.

A separate sleeping cabin is set behind the driver's cab.

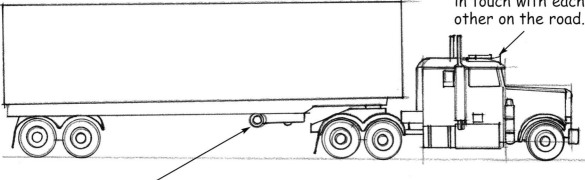

Most trucks today have powerful air brakes on all wheels – and an emergency braking system in case these fail. Brakes are vital on such heavy vehicles.

Radio antennae allow long-distance drivers to report to base or keep in touch with each other on the road.

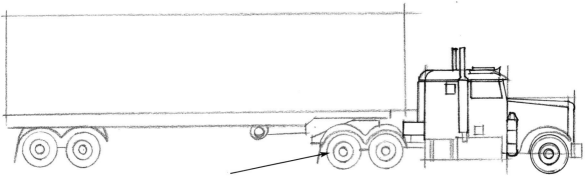

Fold-away parking wheels are lowered to support the trailer when it is uncoupled from the tractor unit.

Tractor-and-trailer outfits like this date back to the mid-1900s. But there have been many improvements since then!

Dump Truck

The dump truck works at building sites, mines, and quarries. It carries heavy loads of rock, earth, and rubble. When, it is time to unload, the body of the truck tips backward to dump this material wherever it is wanted.

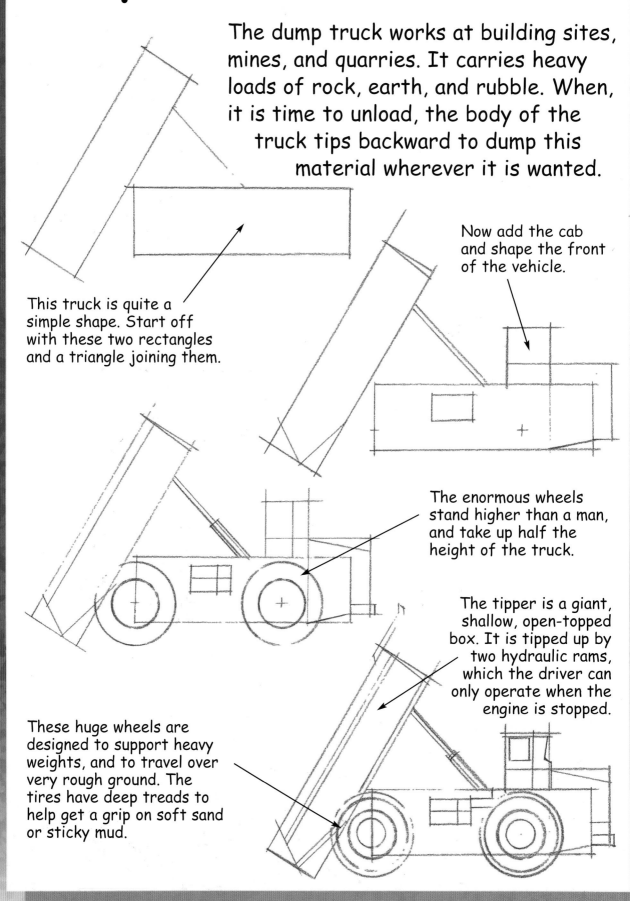

This truck is quite a simple shape. Start off with these two rectangles and a triangle joining them.

Now add the cab and shape the front of the vehicle.

The enormous wheels stand higher than a man, and take up half the height of the truck.

The tipper is a giant, shallow, open-topped box. It is tipped up by two hydraulic rams, which the driver can only operate when the engine is stopped.

These huge wheels are designed to support heavy weights, and to travel over very rough ground. The tires have deep treads to help get a grip on soft sand or sticky mud.

This steel canopy at the front of the tipper helps to stop the load from spilling forward on to the cab.

The driver's cab is perched high above those tall wheels – so he needs a ladder to climb up to his seat.

A narrow platform above the front wheel gives the driver a walkway to his cab.

The back of the tipper slants inward to form a funnel shape, making it easier to direct the load as it slides out.

Draw in the tread patterns of the tires. Dump trucks have the biggest tires of any vehicle, so you need to make them look good and solid.

Giant dump trucks are too big and heavy to drive on roads – they would damage the surface. To carry building materials by road, smaller, lighter versions are used.

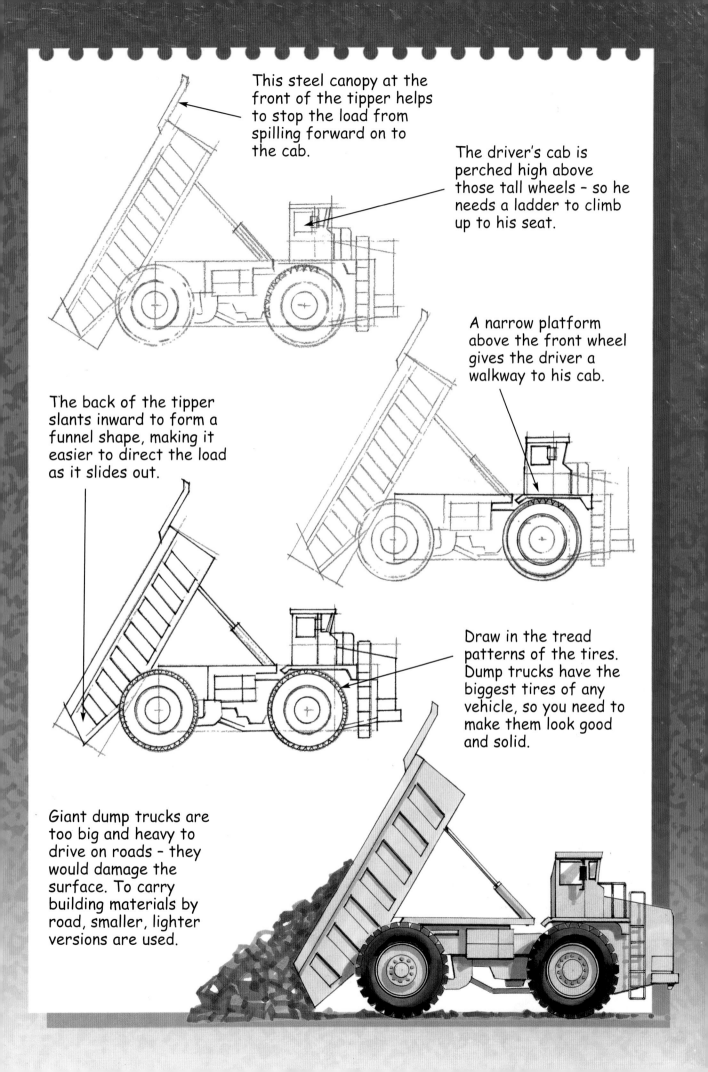

Namecaleb

MEMBER KITCHENS

RECIPES & PROJECTS

Member Kitchens
Recipes & Projects

Mike Vail
Vice President, Product Marketing and
Business Development

Tom Carpenter
Director of Book and New Media Development

Dan Kennedy
Book Production Manager

Heather Koshiol
Book Development Coordinator

Matt Preis
Book Development Assistant

Beowulf Ltd.
Book Design, Production

Mowers Photography
Food Photography

Handyman Club of America
12301 Whitewater Drive
Minnetonka, MN 55343

1 2 3 4 5 6 7 8 / 01 00 99 98
ISBN 1-58159-030-X

CONTENTS

INTRODUCTION

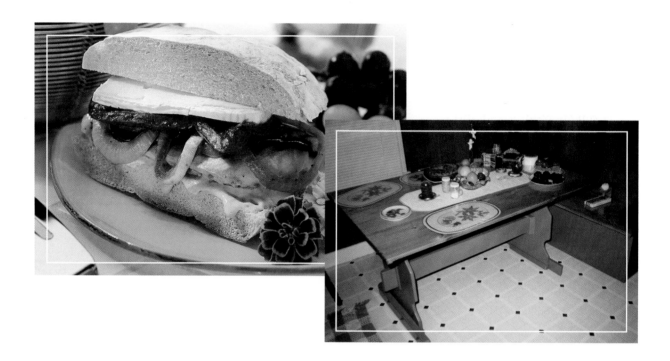

WELCOME TO MEMBER KITCHENS ... AND GREAT RECIPE & PROJECT IDEAS!

When you get right down to it, the kitchen may well be the most lived-in room in your house. Sure, more time is probably spent sleeping in the bedroom. But when you consider cooking, eating, cleaning up, reading the mail, doing bills, having a cup of coffee, discussing family plans and matters ... the kitchen is the central gathering place, where much of the living is happening.

We knew all this as we began creating this member-generated book, and the result you're holding—*Member Kitchens: Recipes & Projects*—is a delight. First and foremost, you get 200 recipes directly from the kitchens of Handyman Club of America members. Once you see—and create—a few of these dishes, you'll realize that your fellow members know how to cook and eat!

And to make sure your kitchen—that most important of gathering places—remains bright, functional, efficient, comfortable and attractive, we've included a selection of members' kitchen improvement projects. Our hope is you'll find some ideas and techniques that will inspire you to make your kitchen even more beautiful and livable.

THE RECIPES

From zucchini bread and salsas to pasties and peach cobbler, the recipe ideas here will make you feel just as at-home as the kitchens do. Along with the great variations on time-honored favorites like those just mentioned, you'll also discover some all-new ideas like Tosatadas Compuestas, Salmon au Pouvre and Refried Bean Cake, just to name a few.

THE PROJECTS

To contemplate a change of kitchen atmosphere, take a tour of the kitchen updating ideas that members have included—from revitalizing a dark kitchen, customizing cabinets and making more storage space, to adding a unique pine-top island with chainlink fencepost legs. Whether you borrow a concept or follow the project step-by-step, the ideas here will get your creative juices flowing.

Enjoy the mix of recipes and projects in *Member Kitchens*. Consider this book a tool—and a beautiful one at that—that you will use in your kitchen and maybe even in your workshop. Both ways, your creations are sure to be big hits.

Sausage Soup

Soups, Breads & Appetizers

SAUSAGE SOUP

1 lb. sweet Italian sausage
1/2 onion, chopped
2 ribs celery, chopped
7 cups water
3/4 cup chopped broccoli
3/4 cup chopped cauliflower
1 carrot, grated
5 medium potatoes, peeled and cubed

7 fresh medium mushrooms,
   chopped (optional)
10 1/2-oz. can cream of mushroom soup
1 T. chicken bouillon granules
2 tsp. garlic powder
1 tsp. onion powder
1/2 tsp. basil
1/2 cup processed American cheese spread

Brown sausage, onion and celery in large soup pot. Add water, broccoli, cauliflower, carrot, potatoes, mushrooms if desired, cream of mushroom soup, bouillon, garlic and onion powders and basil. Simmer slowly, stirring occasionally, for about 2 hours. Add cheese just before serving, stirring to mix well. Serve with garlic bread.

Doris Swihart
Heron, MT

MARK'S ISLAND

My kitchen island table design went through countless revisions until one day I spotted the chain link fence supplies at the local building supply store and inspiration struck. The parts fit together like Tinker Toys, and it was easy to figure out a way to join them into a table base. I had no shortage of options for the tabletop and considered everything from butcher block to ceramic tile to poured concrete. I ended up choosing solid wood. I found a piece of $^5/_4$ Sugar Pine that was 16 in. wide. It also had some fairly extensive spalling occurring in the sapwood that added pattern and color to the board. I surface planed the board then cut it in half and face-glued the pieces together to make the tabletop blank. After the glue had set, I used a $4^1/_2$ in. carpenter's drawknife to shape and round-over the edges. I cut the ends of the tabletop freehand with a jig saw, then used a round micro-plane rasp to shape the ends so they were consistent with the edge profiles. Finally, I sanded the top and coated it with four thin coats of satin polyurethane. I also sealed the underside of the top with a couple of coats of poly.

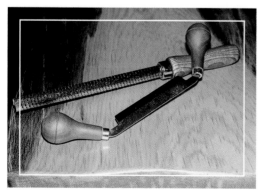

A drawknife and round microplane rasp were used to impart a "wavy" texture to the edges of the tabletop.

To attach the top to the base, I cut plugs from a scrap of the Sugar Pine, using a $2^1/_2$ in. dia. hole saw. Then I marked the positions of the legs onto the underside of the top and attached the plugs to the top with glue and screws. Then it was just a matter of fitting the legs onto the plugs and driving them home with a mallet (the tension fit between the legs and the plugs is important to the stability of the table).

Mark Johanson
Minneapolis, MN

SAUSAGE & POTATO SOUP

3 T. olive oil
2 to 3 onions, chopped
1/4 to 1/2 T. parsley
1 T. fresh or 1 tsp. dried thyme
2 bay leaves

Italian sausage or bratwurst,
    cut into bite-sized pieces
Chicken stock (see below) or water
6 to 8 cups potatoes, cut in wedges
Salt and pepper

Sauté onion in olive oil for 2 to 3 minutes or until onion turns clear. Add parsley, thyme, bay leaves and sausage. Cook for 3 minutes. Add stock (see recipe below) and potatoes. Reduce heat, cover and simmer until potatoes are tender. Salt and pepper to taste.

• CHICKEN STOCK •

1 whole chicken, cut into pieces
2 medium onions
2 ribs celery
1 large carrot

2 T. dried parsley
Bay leaf
1 tsp. thyme
Salt and pepper

Place all ingredients in large pot, adding water to cover all. Bring to a boil. Let simmer until chicken falls from bones. Strain thoroughly.

Kevin Barnett
Troutman, NC

Broccoli Salad

BROCCOLI SALAD

2 bunches broccoli, cut small with no stems
$^1/_2$ lb. bacon, fried crisp
1 cup mild cheddar cheese
$^1/_4$ cup finely chopped red onion
1 cup mayonnaise
$^1/_2$ cup sugar
2 T. cider vinegar

Combine broccoli, bacon, cheddar cheese and onion in large bowl. Mix mayonnaise, sugar and vinegar and pour over broccoli. Stir well. Refrigerate and stir just before serving.

Ken Goerdt
Hibbing, MN

BEST DARN ZUCCHINI BREAD

3 eggs
2 cups sugar
$^1/_2$ cup vegetable oil
$^1/_2$ cup butter or margarine, softened
1 T. vanilla
2 cups grated zucchini
2 cups flour
1 tsp. baking powder
1 tsp. baking soda
1 tsp. salt
1 tsp. cinnamon
1 tsp. lemon rind
1 cup chopped nuts

Beat eggs until light. Add sugar, oil, butter and vanilla; mix. Add zucchini and stir thoroughly. Sift flour, baking powder, baking soda, salt and cinnamon and add to batter; stir until smooth. Add lemon rind and nuts. Pour into 2 greased and floured loaf pans and bake at 350°F for about an hour.

Doris Swihart
Heron, MT

KITCHEN REMODELING

We recently remodeled our 1970s, very dark kitchen, doing all the work ourselves. We had dark oak cabinets, dark floor tile (brown), dark woodwork and furniture. We painted all our cupboards white, used blue crown mouldings and light oak for the rest, including the top of the half wall by the stairway. My husband built the shelf extension hanging from the ceiling and enlarged the cabinets under the counter extension to be much deeper and include the shelves for my cookbooks. We laid ceramic tile on the floor.

Betty & Wayne Terpstra
Littleton, CO

ZUCCHINI BREAD

2/3 cup shortening
2²/3 cup sugar
4 eggs
3 cups shredded zucchini
2/3 cup water
2 tsp. vanilla
3¹/3 cups flour
2 tsp. baking soda
¹/2 tsp. baking powder
1¹/2 tsp. salt
1 tsp. cinnamon
1 tsp. ground cloves
2/3 cup chopped nuts (optional)
2/3 cup raisins (optional)

Mix shortening, sugar, eggs, zucchini, water and vanilla together. Sift flour, baking soda, baking powder, salt, cinnamon and cloves and blend into batter. Stir in nuts and raisins if desired. Pour into two greased loaf pans and bake at 350°F for 1 hour and 10 minutes. Let cool before slicing.

Michael Malek
Parma, OH

FRESH SALSA

4 green chilies, fire
  roasted, sweated,
  peeled, seeded, diced
1 medium white onion,
  finely diced
1 medium red onion,
  finely diced
6 Roma tomatoes, seeded
  and chopped
1 tsp. minced garlic
1 bunch cilantro, finely
  chopped
Juice from 1 lemon
Juice from 2 limes
1 tsp. hot sauce
4 T. tequila (optional)
1 tsp. salt
1 tsp. white pepper

In a large bowl, mix green chiles, onions, tomatoes, garlic, cilantro, juices, hot sauce, tequila, salt and pepper. Chill for 1 hour and serve.

Scott Allen
Henderson, NV

SOUTHERN ICED TEA

1 cup sugar
1 qt. water
Loose tea or 2 large tea bags

Dissolve sugar in water and bring to a boil. Brew tea in pot to desired strength or brew 10 cups in automatic coffee brewer, using tea bags in place of coffee filter. Add sugar water to tea; never add sugar to make sweetened iced tea!

William Leistner
Maryville, TN

CHEESY JALAPEÑO CRACKLIN' CORNBREAD

1 egg, beaten
1³/4 cups milk
3 T. oil
1 T. mayonnaise
¹/2 cup grated cheddar cheese
3 pickled jalapeño peppers, minced

²/3 cup packaged cracklings
1¹/2 cups cornmeal
¹/2 cup flour
1 tsp. baking powder
¹/2 tsp. salt

Combine egg, milk, oil, mayonnaise, cheese, peppers and cracklings. Sift cornmeal, flour, baking powder and salt and add to egg mixture. Beat well and pour into greased pan or iron skillet. Bake at 350°F for 15 to 20 minutes or until toothpick inserted comes out clean.

James Legler
LaGrange, TX

SENATE BEAN SOUP

¹/4 cup butter
1 medium white onion, diced
2 cups navy beans, soaked overnight
¹/4 tsp. liquid smoke

1 tsp. salt
1 ham hock or ham bone with about
 a quarter of meat left on, or 1 cup
 ham, diced

Melt butter in frying pan over medium heat. Add onion and lightly brown. Place soaked beans in large pot with water. Add onion, liquid smoke, salt and ham. Boil gently until beans are tender.

William Leistner
Maryville, TN

Cheesy Jalapeño Cracklin' Cornbread

CASINO BUTTER CLAMS

Clams in the shell, opened and washed
2 cups butter
1 green pepper, finely chopped
1 small jar pimientos, chopped
2 to 3 cloves garlic, minced
Worcestershire sauce to taste
Dash hot sauce
Salt and white pepper to taste
Parsley to taste
Bread crumbs, optional
Chopped bacon

Mix butter, green pepper, pimientos and garlic with Worcestershire sauce, hot sauce, salt and pepper and parsley to taste. Place a pat of casino butter on each clam and sprinkle with bread crumbs if desired. Top with chopped bacon. Broil on cookie sheet until bacon is crisp and clams are hot.

William Kent
Buffalo, NY

ZUCCHINI RELISH

10 cups finely chopped squash
4 cups finely chopped onion
5 T. salt
2¹/₄ cups white vinegar
4 cups sugar
1 tsp. nutmeg
2 tsp. dry mustard
2 tsp. celery seed
2 T. cornstarch
1 red bell pepper, pureed
1 green bell pepper, pureed

Mix squash, onion and salt and let stand overnight; drain and rinse in cold water. Add vinegar, sugar, nutmeg, dry mustard, celery seed, cornstarch and pureed peppers. Cook over low heat for 30 minutes. Makes six pints.

Guy and Evelyn Claypool
Chapparal, NM

PORTUGUESE KALE & POTATO SOUP

2 T. olive oil
1 lb. spicy turkey or chicken sausage
1 medium onion, chopped
3 cloves garlic, minced
6 cups chicken broth

2 medium potatoes, sliced thick
$^1/_4$ tsp. crushed red pepper
1 lb. kale, stems removed
Salt

Heat 1 tablespoon oil in large pot over medium heat; add sausage and cook 5 minutes, stirring to break it up. Transfer sausage to plate. Add remaining 1 tablespoon oil to pot and cook onion until golden brown. Add garlic and cook 1 more minute. Add sausage, broth, potatoes and red pepper and heat to simmer. In bunches, stack kale leaves in piles on a cutting board. Using a long, sharp knife, cut through each pile to make narrow ribbons $^1/_2$ inch wide. Stir shredded kale into soup and simmer about 40 minutes or until kale is tender. Season with salt and additional red pepper to taste.

Fran Goran
Gowanda, NY

SEASONED CHICKEN STRIPS

2 (10-oz.) pkgs. frozen
breaded chicken strips

4 oz. hot sauce
2 T. butter
1 T. chili powder

Mix hot sauce, butter and chili powder in small saucepan over medium heat. When butter is melted, turn heat to low. Deep fry chicken strips according to package directions.

Drain strips on paper towel to remove excess grease. Place seasoning mixture and cooked strips in covered bowl and shake until strips are thoroughly coated. Serve hot with ranch or blue cheese dressing, or with remainder of seasoning mixture.

Jerry Gatewood
Reynoldsburg, OH

BEEFY CHEESE BALL

4-oz. pkg. dried beef,
chopped fine
8-oz. pkg. cream cheese

4 green onions, chopped
fine
1 tsp. Worcestershire sauce
1 T. horseradish sauce

Set aside 2 tablespoons dried beef. Combine remaining beef, cream cheese, onion, Worcestershire sauce and horseradish sauce. Mix well and shape into ball. Sprinkle 2 tablespoons dried beef on wax paper and roll ball in beef until completely covered. Refrigerate overnight. Serve with assorted crackers.

Jerry R. Cramer
Spring Grove, PA

POTATO ROLLS

4 cups bread flour
$^3/_4$ tsp. salt
$^1/_3$ cup sugar
5 T. butter

1 egg
$^3/_4$ cup lukewarm water
$^1/_2$ cup lukewarm mashed
potatoes
2 tsp. dry yeast

Mix flour, salt and sugar and set aside. Melt butter and add egg, water and mashed potatoes. Add yeast. Stir in flour, salt and sugar. Knead well until dough is smooth. Let rise for about 2 hours. Punch down, let rest for 5 minutes, then shape into 2 dozen rolls. Arrange in pan and let rise. Bake at 325°F for 30 to 40 minutes or until golden brown.

Brenda and Paul Watts
Nancy, KY

BEST GARLIC BREAD

1 loaf fresh Italian bread
7 cloves fresh garlic

1 cup butter
Oregano
Parsley

Preheat oven to 350°F. Cut bread into 2-inch, angled slices. Press garlic cloves with garlic press; put garlic juice and pieces in bowl. Melt butter; pour into bowl with garlic. Add oregano and parsley; mix well. Brush tops and sides of bread with butter. (Don't use the brush you used to paint the house with, either!) Bake bread until golden brown.

John Margiotta
Peoria, AZ

DOUBLE-ENTRY ISLAND CABINET

The double-entry island cabinet was custom-built from readily available melamine shelving pieces, hardware from a woodworkers' catalog, glass from a local glass and mirror company, and lighting from our local home improvement warehouse.
We couldn't find such a creation anywhere, at any price, so this was the solution we built.

James Herkcotz
Cape Coral, FL

FOCACCIA À LA EUGENIO

3 envelopes active dry yeast
2 cups warm water (105°F to 115°F)
2 T. sugar
5 to 6 cups unbleached all-purpose flour
1 T. coarse kosher salt

3 T. extra virgin olive oil
$^3/4$ cups thinly sliced purple onion, separated
Several sprigs fresh rosemary, stripped and
   chopped (or $^1/2$ to 2 tsp. dried rosemary)
$^1/2$ to 1 tsp. fresh coarsely ground black pepper

Dissolve yeast in warm water and sugar in medium bowl; let stand in warm place for 10 minutes or until foamy. Mix 5 cups flour with 1$^1/2$ teaspoons salt in large bowl. Pour in yeast mixture and 2 tablespoons olive oil. Stir with wooden spoon, gradually incorporating enough flour to form soft dough. Add flour cautiously, only if dough is too sticky to handle. Sprinkle work surface with $^1/4$ cup flour, turn dough onto surface and sprinkle with $^1/4$ cup flour as needed to prevent sticking. Knead dough for about 10 minutes if kneading by hand; if using mixer, use dough hook for 3 minutes and finish by hand until dough is smooth and elastic. Shape into ball and place in large bowl lightly greased with olive oil. Turn dough to bring greased side up. Cover tightly with plastic wrap and let rise about 30 minutes or until doubled in bulk.

Punch down, cover and let rise again until doubled, again about 30 minutes. Repeat for third time. Transfer dough into greased 11 x 15-inch jelly roll pan. Push dough into rectangular shape, bring it up over edges and roll over slightly to make 1-inch edge, similar to pizza crust. Using knuckles or fingertips, make indentations across surface, staying clear of edges. Cover loosely and let rise about 15 minutes.

In medium mixing bowl, mix remaining 1 tablespoon (or more) olive oil, onion slices, remaining

1$^1/2$ tsp. kosher salt, rosemary and pepper. Press dough again with knuckles as before, avoiding edges. Spread onion mixture over dough, leaving edges clear to receive a brushing with remaining olive oil left in bowl. Bake at 400°F for 35 to 45 minutes. Cover bread if it appears too brown on top.

Remove from oven and cool slightly on wire rack before carefully turning it out of pan. Break or cut pieces to serve. Freezes well when cooled. Reheat smaller pieces in microwave if eaten immediately. Reheat larger sections in oven heated to 400°F and turned off, leaving bread in for 5 minutes to re-crisp.

Gene Brown
Raleigh, NC

NEW ORLEANS GUMBO

1¹/₂ to 2 lbs. boneless chicken, diced
1 pkg. andouille sausage, diced
2 pkgs. kielbasa, diced
1 cup butter
1 cup flour
1 large onion, diced
1 large bell pepper, diced
1 lb. carrots, diced
1 bunch celery, diced
3 cloves garlic, diced
2 (48-oz.) cans chicken broth
¹/₃ cup soy sauce
3 T. parsley flakes
Salt and pepper

Melt butter in very large pot on low heat and slowly stir in flour. Continue stirring 20 to 25 minutes, until mixture turns the color of peanut butter. Add onion, bell pepper, carrots, celery and garlic and mix. Cover pot and cook on low for 5 to 10 minutes.

Add chicken, sausage, kielbasa, chicken broth, soy sauce, parsley flakes, salt and pepper to taste. Bring to a boil, stirring to prevent sticking. Reduce heat to low, cover and simmer for 4 to 5 hours, stirring occasionally and adding salt and pepper if necessary.

Susan Sacks
Coplay, PA

OATMEAL BREAD

2 cups rolled oats, regular or quick-cooking
3 cups water
1 T. yeast
¹/₂ cup warm water
¹/₄ cup packed brown sugar
1 tsp. salt
¹/₄ cup molasses
¹/₃ cup shortening, melted
5 to 6 cups flour
¹/₂ cup walnuts (optional)

Cook oats in water and let cool. Dissolve yeast in ¹/₂ cup warm water and set aside. Mix brown sugar, salt, molasses and shortening. Add dissolved yeast to sugar mixture. When oats have cooled to warm (115°F), add to sugar and yeast mixture. Add enough flour to make a stiff dough; knead until smooth on a floured board. Place in a greased bowl, cover and let rise until double in size.

Knead again for about 5 minutes and add walnuts if desired. Divide dough in two and shape into balls. Cover and let rest 15 minutes. Shape into loaves, brush with oil and roll in rolled oats. Place in two greased loaf pans and let rise until double in volume. Bake at 350°F for 45 to 55 minutes until loaves sound hollow when tapped.

Tim Graham
Moab, UT

Favorite Taco Dip

FAVORITE TACO DIP

8-oz. pkg. cream cheese
16-oz. carton sour cream
1 packet taco seasoning
Shredded lettuce
Diced onion
Diced tomato
Sliced black olives

Mix cream cheese, sour cream and taco seasoning thoroughly; spread on bottom of serving dish. Layer shredded lettuce over cheese and sour cream mixture; follow with layers of onion, tomato and black olives and cheese. Serve with tortilla chips.

Jill and Joel Ramthun
Litchfield, MN

LOW-FAT ZUCCHINI BREAD

1 cup applesauce
2 cups sugar
2 cups grated zucchini
3 tsp. vanilla
3 eggs, beaten
3 cups flour

1 tsp. salt
$1^1/_4$ tsp. baking powder
1 tsp. baking soda
3 tsp. cinnamon
1 cup nuts (optional)

Mix applesauce, sugar, zucchini and vanilla. Add beaten eggs. Sift flour, salt, baking powder, baking soda and cinnamon and add to batter. Add more flour, if necessary, to make batter slightly thicker than cake batter. Stir in nuts if desired. Pour into 2 well-greased loaf pans and bake at 350°F for 1 hour or until toothpick inserted comes out clean.

Denise Kidman
Roy, UT

SUN-DRIED (OVEN-DRIED) TOMATOES

2 to 3 lbs. ripe roma tomatoes
Fresh rosemary
Extra virgin olive oil

Split tomatoes in half lengthwise, arrange on wire cooling racks, cut side up, and sprinkle with salt. Place racks of tomatoes on baking sheets to catch drippings. Bake at 180°F to 200°F for about 8 hours.

Change pan positions every couple of hours and watch closely after 6 or 7 hours to make certain no pieces become too dry. When dried to leathery and pliant texture, place in very clean canning jar, add 2 to 3 sprigs fresh rosemary and fill jar to top with extra virgin olive oil. Store at room temperature for 1 month in dark place before using.

Gene Brown
Raleigh, NC

FRESH VEGGIE SALSA

1 envelope Italian salad dressing mix
12 large tomatoes, chopped
3 green onions, chopped
1 large onion, chopped
3 green peppers, chopped
1 rib celery, chopped
$^1/_4$ cup tomato juice
1 T. lemon juice
2 T. cooking oil
2 T. vinegar
1 T. ground cumin
$^1/_4$ to $^1/_2$ tsp. crushed red pepper, optional
Hot pepper sauce
1 pkg. fruit pectin

Combine dressing mix, tomatoes, onions, peppers, celery, juices, oil, vinegar, cumin and crushed red pepper (if desired). Sprinkle with hot pepper sauce to taste; thicken with fruit pectin. Stir well and refrigerate for 2 hours or overnight. Serve with tortilla chips.

Ken Goerdt
Hibbing, MN

SHRIMP SPREAD

$4^1/_2$-oz. can tiny shrimp, rinsed and drained
3 oz. grated cheddar cheese
2 T. green onion, chopped
2 hard cooked eggs, grated (optional)
Mayonnaise to taste

Combine shrimp, cheese, onion and eggs with enough mayonnaise to make mixture smooth. Chill. Serve with crackers.

William Kent
Buffalo, NY

EVELYN'S CHILI CON QUESO

2 lbs. processed American cheese
14-oz. can condensed milk
2 (4-oz) cans chopped chili peppers
14-oz. can diced tomatoes, drained
Garlic salt to taste

Melt cheese in milk over low heat. Add peppers, tomatoes and garlic salt and mix well. Serve warm.

Guy Claypool
Chapparal, NM

MOLASSES WHEAT BREAD

$^1/_4$ cup molasses
$^1/_4$ cup honey
2 pkgs. dry yeast
$1^3/_4$ cups warm water
$^2/_3$ cup nonfat dry milk powder
2 eggs, beaten
2 T. cooking oil

$1^1/_2$ tsp. salt
$^1/_2$ cup quick-cooking or rolled oats
$^1/_2$ cup wheat germ
$^1/_2$ cup whole bran cereal
2 cups whole-wheat flour
1 cup bread flour
$2^1/_2$ to $3^1/_2$ cups all-purpose flour

Combine molasses, honey and yeast in warm water and let stand 10 minutes or until foamy. Stir in powdered milk, eggs, oil and salt. Stir in oats, wheat germ and cereal. Beat in whole wheat and bread flour. Stir in enough all-purpose flour to make moderately stiff dough. Knead on floured surface for 6 to 8 minutes or until smooth textured. Cover and let rise until doubled in size.

Halve the dough and let it rest for 10 minutes. Shape into 2 loaves and place in greased loaf pans. Cover and let rise until doubled. Bake at 350°F for about 40 minutes or until they sound hollow when tapped.

Doris Swihart
Heron, MT

WATTS' ZUCCHINI BREAD

4 eggs
2 cups sugar
1 cup cooking oil
1 tsp. vanilla

2 cups all-purpose flour
2 cup shredded zucchini
1 cup walnuts

Beat eggs until golden yellow. Add sugar, cooking oil and vanilla and beat until lemon colored and well mixed. Fold in flour. Add zucchini and nuts; mix well. Pour into 2 loaf pans and bake at 350°F for 1 hour.

Brenda and Paul Watts
Nancy, KY

WILD RICE SOUP

1 lb. bacon
1 large onion, chopped
1 lb. fresh mushrooms, sliced
$^1/_2$ cup wild rice
$10^1/_2$-oz. can chicken broth
$10^1/_2$-oz. can cream of potato soup
2 cups milk
1 can chunk chicken
8 oz. processed American cheese

Sauté bacon in large skillet. Remove bacon and sauté onion and mushrooms in bacon grease. Do not drain. Bring 5 quarts water and wild rice to boil. Remove from heat and let stand 1 hour.

Add chicken broth, potato soup, milk, chunk chicken and sautéed ingredients to rice. Simmer until rice opens and fluffs, stirring occasionally. Add cheese, heating just enough to melt.

Ken Goerdt
Hibbing, MN

ZUCCHINI APPETIZER SQUARES

4 cups thinly sliced zucchini
$^1/_2$ cup finely chopped onion
1 cup buttermilk baking mix
4 eggs, slightly beaten
$^1/_2$ cup vegetable oil
$^1/_2$ cup Parmesan cheese
2 T. chopped fresh parsley
1 clove garlic, minced
$^1/_2$ tsp. oregano
$^1/_2$ tsp. seasoned salt
pepper to taste

Mix all ingredients in large bowl. Spread in buttered 9 x 13-inch glass pan. Bake at 350°F for 30 minutes or until golden brown and toothpick inserted in center comes out clean. Cut into 1-inch squares.

William Kent
Buffalo, NY

GERMAN POTATO BEAN SOUP

6 to 7 large potatoes, cubed
1 large onion, diced
1 cup diced celery
4 chicken bouillon cubes
4 cups water
2 cups cubed ham or 1 lb. bacon,
browned and drained
8-oz. jar processed cheese spread
2 (28-oz.) cans kidney beans
1/2 pint cream

Combine potatoes, onion, celery, bouillon, and water in slow cooker. Cook on low for 8 hours or overnight until potatoes are tender. Add ham or browned bacon, cheese spread, beans and cream. Heat thoroughly and serve hot.

Ken Goerdt
Hibbing, MN

OVERNIGHT CINNAMON BUNS

2 loaves frozen bread dough, still frozen
1/2 cup nuts (optional)
1/2 cup raisins (optional)
4.6-oz. pkg vanilla pudding (not instant)
2 tsp. cinnamon
1 cup brown sugar
2 T. milk
1/2 cup butter, melted

Grease 9 x 13-inch pan and line bottom with nuts and raisins if desired. Cut frozen bread dough into small chunks with scissors and arrange in pan. Mix vanilla pudding, cinnamon, brown sugar, milk and butter to make thick mixture. Pour over bread chunks. Cover and refrigerate overnight.

Bake, uncovered, at 350°F for 30 minutes. Cool 5 to 10 minutes and flip pan upside down to remove buns.

Tina Holschbach
Newton, WI

SALSA VERDE

6 fresh, ripe avocados
6 fresh medium tomatoes, finely diced
2 medium white onions, finely diced
2 medium red onions, finely diced
2 small can green chiles, diced with juice
1 bunch fresh cilantro, finely chopped
4 T. lemon juice
4 T. tomato juice
2 tsp. hot sauce
$1^1/2$ tsp. salt
1 tsp. white pepper
1 tsp. sugar

Peel ripe avocados and cut into $^1/_8$-inch cubes; place in large bowl. Add tomatoes, onions, green chiles, cilantro, lemon and tomato juices, hot sauce, salt, pepper and sugar. Stir thoroughly and chill for 1 hour before serving.

Scott Allen
Henderson, NV

BANANA BREAD

$^1/2$ cup butter or margarine, room temperature
$^3/4$ cup sugar
2 eggs
1 cup all-purpose flour
1 tsp. baking soda
$^1/2$ tsp. salt
1 cup whole wheat flour
3 large ripe bananas, mashed
1 tsp. vanilla
$^1/2$ cup coarsely chopped walnuts

Cream butter and sugar until light and fluffy. Add eggs, one at a time, beating well each time. Sift all-purpose flour, baking soda and salt. Stir in whole wheat flour and add to creamed mixture. Mix well. Fold in mashed bananas, vanilla and walnuts. Pour into greased 9 x 5 x 3-inch loaf pan and bake at 350°F for 50 to 60 minutes or until toothpick inserted in middle comes out clean. Cool in pan for 10 minutes, then cool on rack.

Linda G. Lilley
Farmville, VA

PESTO

3 oz. fresh basil or 1 T. dried basil
1/3 cup olive oil
6 cloves garlic, minced

1/2 cup grated Parmesan cheese
1 T. butter
3 oz. fresh spinach (if using dried basil)

Place dried basil (if using), olive oil, garlic, cheese and butter in small bowl and mix well. Chop fresh basil or spinach into fine pieces; add to bowl and mix well. Refrigerate until ready to serve. Serve in soups, pasta, scrambled eggs, or as a quick spread for garlic bread.

Gary Mallon
Post Falls, ID

IOWA CORN CHOWDER

1 lb. ham, diced
4 potatoes, diced
1 onion, diced
1 green pepper, diced
14 3/4-oz. can cream-style corn

15 1/4-oz. can whole kernel corn
1 can lima beans
2 cups milk
Salt and pepper

Cover ham, potatoes, onion and green pepper with water in 4-quart pot. Bring to boil and simmer until tender. Add cream-style corn, whole kernel corn, lima beans, and milk and heat until near boiling. Do not let milk boil! Add salt and pepper to taste. May be thickened with flour if desired.

Sterling Rachwal
Winnebago, WI

Ralph's Special Rice

SIDES & SALADS

RALPH'S SPECIAL RICE

2 cups uncooked rice
4 cups chicken or beef broth
2 to 3 red, yellow or green peppers, chopped
$^{1}/_{2}$ cup chopped hot peppers
1 large onion, chopped
8 oz. hot sausage, chopped
8 oz. mild sausage, chopped

Cook rice in broth, adding water if needed, until rice is done but still slightly moist. Sauté peppers, onion and sausages in large skillet until thoroughly cooked. Add to rice and mix well.

Ralph J. Messuri
Elyria, OH

BROCCOLI POLONAISE

5 lbs. broccoli
2 tsp. salt
16 cups water
1 cup dry bread crumbs
2 cups butter or margarine, melted
3 eggs, hard-boiled and chopped
Fresh chopped parsley

Boil broccoli, uncovered, in salted water until tender. Place in large serving dish. Brown bread crumbs in butter. Spread 1/2 cup browned bread crumbs over broccoli. Garnish with chopped eggs and parsley.

Variations: Use cauliflower, Brussels sprouts, asparagus or carrots in place of broccoli.

Alton E. Mickle
Birmingham, AL

SCALLOPED POTATOES

3 T. butter, melted
1/2 cup chopped onion
3 T. flour
1/2 tsp. salt
Pepper
1 1/2 cups milk
4 large potatoes
Shredded cheese (optional)

Combine melted butter and onion. Blend flour, salt, pepper and add milk a little at a time to prevent lumps. Add butter and onions and microwave on high for 5 to 7 minutes until thick. Add potatoes to sauce. Cover and microwave on high for 13 to 15 minutes, stirring once. Add shredded cheese if desired.

Gladys Jackson
Hershey, NE

DALE'S BAKED BEANS

2 large cans pork and beans
1 cup brown sugar
2 tsp. Worcestershire sauce
14-oz. bottle ketchup
1 lb. bacon
2 medium onions, chopped
2 medium green peppers

Mix pork and beans with brown sugar, Worcestershire sauce and ketchup in slow cooker turned to high heat. Cut bacon into 1-inch pieces and fry until about $2/3$ done; partially drain grease. Sauté onion and pepper in remaining grease until slightly soft. Drain and add to bean mixture. Reduce heat to low and cook $1^1/2$ to 2 hours, stirring occasionally. If thicker beans are desired, partially drain sauce from pork and beans before mixing ingredients.

Dale Anderson
West Valley, UT

SPAGHETTI SALAD

1 lb. spaghetti, cooked and drained
1 cucumber, quartered and chopped
1 green pepper, chopped
2 tomatoes, chopped
4 green onions, chopped
$1/2$ to 1 cup Parmesan cheese
$2^1/4$-oz. can sliced black olives
16-oz. bottle Italian dressing

Mix spaghetti, cucumber, green pepper, tomatoes, onions, Parmesan cheese and black olives. Add enough dressing to coat pasta and vegetables. Refrigerate overnight before serving.

Lesa and Mark Kilpatrick
Warren, AR

WALL-HUNG OPEN STORAGE UNIT

The end wall of this corridor-type kitchen was essentially useless for cabinetry because the two opposing doors created a traffic zone. The only space available was the 4" depth of the door jambs and trim. Corridor kitchens can be very tight on space and this one was no exception. What was needed was a workable and attractive way to use this wall for storage within the minimal allowable space.

The solution, which has proven to be very effective over the years and has survived two separate kitchen remodels, was to create this special unit which hangs on the wall from the baseboard to ceiling. Approximately 7' high and 8' wide, it provides plenty of space on the lower adjustable shelves for staples and condiments which are used regularly for cooking, and it is always easy to tell at a glance which item is running low.

The upper portion has recessed, laminate-covered panels, allowing easy access to many pots, pans and other cooking gadgets that are used regularly. A major bonus is that this unit and all the things on it visually enrich the appearance of the kitchen and cut down on countertop clutter.

Construction is of ³/₄" birch plywood with solid birch edging, finished with polyurethane, with plastic laminate facing on the recessed back panels. The white grids come with special pop-on hangers to accommodate different types of gadgets.

Gene Brown
Raleigh, NC

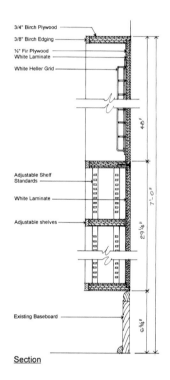

3/4" Birch Plywood
3/8" Birch Edging
1/2" Fir Plywood
White Laminate
White Heller Grid

Adjustable Shelf Standards

White Laminate

Adjustable shelves

Existing Baseboard

__Section__

RAATIKA — FINNISH RUTABAGA COLD DISH

1 medium size rutabaga (about 2 lbs.)
1/2 cup sugar
1 1/2 tsp. cinnamon
2 slices white bread
1 cup cream or condensed milk

Clean, dice and cook rutabaga in salted water, then mash. Soak bread in cream and, if desired, mix in blender to smooth. Mix sugar, cinnamon and soaked bread with rutabaga mash. Pour into 2-quart casserole and bake at 350°F for 15 minutes. Refrigerate before eating.

Marty Aalto
LaGrange, GA

VERY EASY BAKED BEANS

2 (28-oz.) cans baked beans, any flavor
1/2 cup chopped green bell pepper
1/2 cup chopped onion
1/3 cup packed brown sugar
1 cup pineapple chunks
1 lb. Kielbasa sausage cut into 1-inch pieces

Mix beans, green pepper, onion, brown sugar and pineapple in casserole. Bake at 400°F for 15 minutes. Place meat on top on edge, making two rows. Bake for another 15 minutes. Serve either hot or cold.

Sally and James Miner
Mohawk, NY

BROCCOLI PARMESAN

5 lbs. fresh broccoli
8 cups cheddar cheese sauce
24 oz. seasoned bread crumbs

Trim broccoli and cut into serving pieces, leaving 4 inches of stem in place. Steam broccoli until barely done and arrange in ovenproof serving pan. Top broccoli with cheddar cheese sauce and seasoned crumbs and bake at 350°F for 10 to 15 minutes or until crumbs are golden brown. Garnish and serve.

James Mullen
East Meredith, NY

HUSH PUPPIES

1 cup yellow cornmeal
1 cup flour
1 heaping tsp. baking powder
1 tsp. salt
1 egg
14 3/4-oz. can creamed corn
6 jalapeño peppers, chopped fine (optional)
3 green onions, chopped fine
Water

Mix all ingredients with enough water to form balls. Drop by tablespoon into hot oil and fry until golden. Serve with fried fish.

Curtis L. Norris
Magnolia, MS

SPICY SOUTHWESTERN SALAD

1 cup elbow or shell macaroni
15¹/₄-oz. can whole-kernel corn
¹/₄ tsp. salt
¹/₂ tsp. pepper
1 tsp. garlic powder
1 tsp. onion powder
1 tsp. cilantro
1 tsp. lemon juice

¹/₂ tsp. Worcestershire
15-oz. can garbanzo beans
16-oz. can kidney beans
1 cup diced celery
1 cup diced onion
1 can diced tomatoes with jalapeños
1 can tomatoes and green chiles

Cook macaroni according to package directions, then cool. Drain corn, reserving liquid in small bowl. Stir salt, pepper, garlic powder, onion powder, cilantro, lemon juice and Worcestershire sauce into corn liquid. Drain garbanzo beans and kidney beans; rinse with corn in cold water. Pour into large bowl and mix in macaroni, celery, onion, tomatoes and small bowl of spiced corn liquid. Serve chilled.

Jim Neidigh
Fallon, NV

CHEESY POTATOES

3 to 5 round white or red potatoes
4 T. butter margarine
1 small onion, chopped

Salt and pepper to taste
¹/₂ lb. cheddar cheese, shredded

Wash potatoes (or peel if desired) and slice. Layer in 8 x 10-inch cake pan for baking or place on aluminum foil for grilling. Slice butter into pats and set on potatoes. Sprinkle with chopped onion and season with salt and pepper.

Cover pan with aluminum foil or wrap aluminum foil packet tight for grilling. Bake or grill at 325°F for 30 to 45 minutes. Cover potatoes with cheese and cook 5 more minutes.

Rhonda Bahr
Medford, WI

Spicy Southwestern Salad

TABLE & BENCHES

My mother- and father-in-law have wanted a new table and benches to go in their kitchen for some time. I gave this set to them as a Christmas present this past year.

They had told me that they wanted to have benches with seats that lift off and up to create a storage area. I made the table out of pine. The top has been stained and finished with three coats of polyurethane. The bench bases are made of ³/₄" plywood sanded lightly between coats. The seats and backrests are made of pine.

I made the design using measurements and input my in-laws provided, and according to the area the set would occupy in their kitchen. I've made some small things for them in the past, but with this they were very surprised and pleased.

Herb Hankins
Norfolk, VA

SWEET POTATO BALLS

23-oz. can sweet potatoes
2 T. butter or margarine
1 tsp. cinnamon
1 tsp. nutmeg
10-oz. bag large marshmallows
2 pkgs. saltine crackers, crushed
Shortening for deep frying

Heat sweet potatoes until warm. Add butter and spices and mash. Cool potatoes. Roll marshmallows in hand to remove some air; roll each marshmallow in potato mixture until completely coated. Roll in cracker crumbs until well coated. Deep fry in shortening until cracker coating is browned. Drain and serve while warm.

Guy and Evelyn Claypool
Chapparal, NM

GREAT CAESAR!

1 or 2 cloves garlic, crushed
$^1/_3$ cup vegetable oil
2 qts. romaine lettuce
$^1/_2$ cup olive oil
$1^1/_2$ cups dry bread cubes
$^1/_2$ tsp. salt
Freshly ground black pepper
2 eggs, boiled and chopped
$^1/_4$ cup lemon juice
4 to 6 anchovy fillets, chopped (optional)
$^1/_2$ cup grated Parmesan cheese

Combine garlic and oil; let stand at room temperature for 10 minutes or so. Wash lettuce and tear into pieces; place in large bowl lined with paper towels, cover and chill. Brown bread cubes in 3 tablespoons of garlic oil.

Remove paper towels from bowl. Salt and pepper greens, pour remaining garlic oil on greens and toss. Add eggs and lemon juice; toss well. Sprinkle on anchovies and cheese; toss lightly. Add browned bread cubes and toss just until mixed. Serve immediately on chilled plates.

William Kent
Buffalo, NY

WISCONSIN SCRAMBLED EGGS

1 tsp. vegetable oil
3 5- to 6-inch soft shell tortillas,
   cut into strips
1 small onion, chopped
8 eggs
$^1/_4$ cup milk

Salt and pepper
$^1/_2$ cup shredded cheese, any kind
Cooked ham, bacon or pork
   sausages
   (optional)
Favorite toppings

Heat oil in skillet over high heat. Cook tortilla strips and onion about 5 minutes, stirring frequently until strips are crisp. Beat eggs and milk with salt and pepper to taste in mixing bowl. Pour over tortilla mixture and add meat. Reduce heat to medium. Do not stir. As mixture begins to set at bottom and side, gently lift cooked portions with spatula so thin, uncooked portions can flow to the bottom. Shut off heat. Top with cheese and cover for about 2 minutes or until cheese is melted. Top with taco sauce, sour cream, salsa or other favorite seasoning.

Rhonda Bahr
Medford, WI

RANCH BEANS

2 lbs. ground beef
3 medium onions, chopped
1 lb. bacon

3 (15-oz.) cans butter beans
3 (10$^3/_4$-oz.) cans tomato soup
$^3/_4$ cup loosely packed brown sugar

Brown ground beef and onion; drain. Fry bacon until medium crisp. Drain beans, reserving liquid. Mix ground beef and onion with bacon, beans, tomato soup and brown sugar. Bake, uncovered, at 350°F for 1 hour, adding bean broth as needed to retain moisture during baking.

Russell Delancey
Leavittsburg, OH

CORN-STUFFING BALLS

¹/₂ cup chopped onion
1 cup chopped celery
¹/₄ cup margarine
13-oz. can creamed corn
1 cup water
1 tsp. salt
¹/₄ tsp. pepper
¹/₄ tsp. thyme
8-oz. pkg. bread stuffing
3 eggs, lightly beaten
¹/₃ cup melted margarine

Sauté onion and celery in margarine until tender. Add creamed corn, water, salt, pepper and thyme and stir. Pour mixture over bread stuffing and toss lightly. Add beaten eggs and mix. Shape into 12 balls. Place in shallow baking pan and drizzle with melted margarine. Bake at 375°F for 15 minutes.

Hilda Hoffmann
Preston, MN

CABBAGE ROLLS

Large cabbage leaves
Water for blanching
2 T. oil or shortening
1 cup chopped green onion
¹/₂ cup chopped fresh parsley
¹/₂ T. minced garlic
¹/₂ lb. lean ground pork
2 cups cooked rice
Salt to taste
Hot sauce to taste
2 large eggs, beaten
2 cups tomato or vegetable juice

Boil enough water in a large pot to cover cabbage leaves. Blanch leaves until soft, about 5 minutes. Heat oil in a large skillet over medium heat. Sauté onion and parsley. After juice has accumulated, add garlic and continue cooking until onion is tender. Add meat and brown. Stir in cooked rice, salt and hot sauce. Remove from heat, pour into large bowl.

When mixture is cool, add eggs. Place 2 heaping tablespoons of stuffing into each leaf, roll up and secure with toothpicks if necessary. Place close together in baking dish and cover lightly with tomato juice. Bake at 325°F for 30 to 45 minutes.

Guy and Evelyn Claypool
Chapparal, NM

THREE-BEAN BAKED BEANS

8 oz. bacon, diced
8 oz. ground beef
1 large onion, chopped
16-oz. can butter beans, drained
16-oz. can kidney beans, drained
31-oz. can pork and beans
$^{1}/_{2}$ cup sugar

$^{1}/_{2}$ cup brown sugar
$^{1}/_{4}$ cup ketchup
$^{1}/_{4}$ cup barbecue sauce
2 tsp. prepared mustard
2 tsp. molasses
$^{1}/_{2}$ tsp. chili powder
1 tsp. black pepper

Brown bacon, beef and onion; drain and transfer to baking dish. Add three kinds of beans, sugars, ketchup, barbecue sauce, mustard, molasses, chili powder and pepper. Mix well and bake at 350°F for 1 hour.

James Toth
Elgin, IL

CREAMY OVEN-BAKED POTATOES

8 large potatoes, shredded
(or frozen hash-browns)
2 cups whipping cream

2 cups half-and-half
1 tsp. salt
Dash of pepper

Rinse potatoes well after shredding until water runs clear. Place in 9 x 13-inch pan. Mix cream with half-and-half and salt and pepper. Pour cream mixture over potatoes. Bake at 350°F for 1 hour.

Glen Kadelbach
Hutchinson, MN

BAKED ONIONS

2 large onions
2 T. white wine
1 T. margarine, melted
1 T. balsamic vinegar (no substitutes)
1 tsp. fresh chopped parsley
or ¹/₂ tsp. favorite dried herbs
Salt and pepper to taste

Cut top and bottom from onions. Place onions in 2-quart covered casserole. Combine white wine, margarine, balsamic vinegar and parsley in small bowl. Pour over onions. Sprinkle with salt and pepper.

Cover and bake at 375°F for 45 to 50 minutes. Baste with liquid halfway through cooking time. To serve, halve onions and pour liquid over.

Sally and James Miner
Mohawk, NY

CREAMED POTATOES

3 to 5 round white or red potatoes
Milk
4 T. butter or margarine
Salt and pepper to taste
¹/₄ cup milk
2 T. cornstarch

Peel and cut potatoes into pieces and boil in salted water until soft. Drain. Add enough milk to kettle so that potatoes are not quite covered. Add butter and season with salt and pepper. Bring to a boil over medium heat. Dissolve cornstarch in ¹/₄ cup milk, add to potatoes and stir until thickened.

Rhonda Bahr
Medford, WI

SCALLOPED SWEET POTATOES & APPLES

5 lbs. sweet potatoes
2^1/$_2$ lbs. apples, fresh, cored, cut in ^{1}/$_2$-inch slices
1 cup brown sugar
^{1}/$_3$ cup butter
1 T. salt

Wash potatoes and place in large saucepan; cover with water and cook until tender. Peel potatoes and cut into ^{1}/$_2$-inch slices. Layer potato and apple slices alternately in baking dishes.

Combine brown sugar, butter, salt and 1 cup water; cook over low heat, stirring constantly, until sugar is dissolved and syrup is smooth. Pour equally over potatoes and apples in each dish.

Bake at 350°F for 1 hour or until apples are tender.

Alton E. Mickle
Birmingham, AL

POTATO SALAD WITH GREEN ONION DRESSING

POTATO SALAD

12 medium potatoes
18 hard-boiled eggs
$^3/_4$ cup finely chopped onion
$^3/_4$ cup finely chopped celery
$^3/_4$ cup finely chopped green pepper
2 T. prepared yellow mustard
3 tsp. salt
4 tsp. ground cayenne pepper
$^3/_4$ tsp. ground white pepper

GREEN ONION DRESSING

4 whole eggs
3 egg yolks
3 $^1/_3$ cups vegetable oil
$1^1/_2$ cups finely chopped green onion
$4^1/_2$ T. brown mustard
4 T. Dijon-style mustard
4 T. white vinegar
$^1/_4$ lemon, squeezed
2 T. sugar
$^3/_4$ tsp. salt
$^1/_2$ tsp. white pepper

Cook, peel and dice potatoes. Add eggs, onion, celery, green pepper, mustard, salt and pepper. Toss and refrigerate.

Prepare dressing: Whisk eggs and egg yolks until frothy, about 4 minutes. Gradually add oil, whisking constantly. When mixture is thick and creamy, add green onion, mustards, vinegar, lemon juice, sugar, salt and pepper. Refrigerate until ready to use.

Before serving, spoon green onion dressing over salad and serve.

James Mullen
East Meredith, NY

OAK STORAGE CABINET

For Valentine's Day my boyfriend, Doug Becker, made me this beautiful handcrafted oak kitchen storage cabinet that he designed himself. He made the cabinet in his single stall garage that he has converted into a small workshop. He used some of his own tools, including a table saw, miter box saw and router, as well as some tools he borrowed from his employer, where he works as a finish carpenter.

He converted the table-saw table into a router table, which he used to make the cabinet doors. After much sanding, he stained all the pieces and put the cabinet together. For the final touches he applied tung oil, installed shelves in both the top and bottom, and attached brass hardware. The entire project, from design to the finish, took about three weeks.

Jennifer O'Neill
Davenport, IA

CHILE CON CARNE IN TOSTADAS COMPUESTAS

1 lb. lean pork
1 T. flour
1 cup thick red chili sauce
$^{1}/_{2}$ cup tomato juice or water
$^{1}/_{2}$ tsp. garlic salt
1 tsp. ground cumin

$^{1}/_{2}$ tsp. oregano
$^{1}/_{2}$ tsp. salt
Beans
Shredded lettuce
Chopped tomato
Grated cheese

Cut pork into $^{1}/_{2}$-inch squares and fry over low heat until brown and moderately dry. If necessary, drain off all but 2 tablespoons of fat. Add flour and mix well. Add tomato juice or water, red chili sauce and salt. Add water if thinner consistency is desired. Add ground cumin, oregano and garlic salt. Simmer until pork is completely done, about 10 minutes.

• TOSTADAS •

Corn tortillas
Fat for deep frying

Cut 4 1-inch slits evenly spaced around each tortilla. Fry tortilla in deep fat, holding the tortilla down in the center with the flat end of a round wooden roller or a soup ladle. Fry until crisp, then drain on a paper towel.

To assemble Compuestas, place two heaping tablespoons of chili con carne in the tostada. Add beans and garnish with shredded lettuce, chopped tomatoes and grated cheese.

Guy and Evelyn Claypool
Chapparal, NM

Chile con Carne in
Tostadas Compuestas

SIX-SHOOTER BEANS

2 (14-oz.) cans baked beans, ranch-style
   pinto beans or navy beans
1/2 cup chopped onion
2 T. bacon fat, melted
1/4 cup ketchup
4 T. Worcestershire sauce
2 cloves garlic, crushed
3 T. molasses
1 T. vinegar

1 T. chili powder
1 to 3 tsp. hot sauce
1 tsp. yellow mustard (optional)
4 T. strong coffee (optional)
1 or 2 chiles or chipotles, minced (optional)
1 tsp. liquid smoke flavoring (optional)
4 T. brown sugar (optional)
1 large onion, sliced into rings
4 strips bacon

Drain beans well and place in large bowl. In separate bowl, mix chopped onion, bacon fat, ketchup, Worcestershire sauce, garlic, molasses, vinegar, chili powder, hot sauce and optional ingredients. Pour mixture over beans, or use Six-Shooter Sauce (plain or Texas style) below. Transfer to loaf pan and top with onion slices and bacon strips. Bake at 350°F for 45 minutes to 1 hour until top is crusty and center is hot and bubbly.

Kelly Kutz
North St. Petersburg, FL

SIX-SHOOTER SAUCE

1 T. corn oil
2 large onions, finely chopped
1 to 4 serrano peppers, chopped
1 to 4 chipotle peppers, chopped (optional)
6 to 12 cloves garlic, minced
³/4 cup Worcestershire
³/4 cup strong black coffee
¹/3 cup dark molasses
¹/4 cup cider vinegar
¹/4 cup lemon juice
¹/4 cup chili powder
2 T. yellow salad mustard
1¹/2 tsp. ground cumin
1¹/2 tsp. salt

Heat oil in large saucepan over medium heat and sauté onions and serrano peppers until translucent. Add garlic and chipotle peppers and sauté for 2 minutes. Lower heat and add Worcestershire sauce, coffee, molasses, vinegar, lemon juice, chili powder, mustard, cumin and salt. Stir to mix completely and simmer slowly over low heat for 1 hour. Do not boil, as sauce will caramelize and change flavor. Add water if sauce seems too thick.

Kelly Kutz
North St. Petersburg, FL

SIX-SHOOTER SAUCE, TEXAS STYLE

¹/4 cup cider vinegar
3 T. lemon juice
4 or more cloves garlic, minced
2 cups butter or margarine, softened
2 T. dry mustard
¹/3 cup Worcestershire sauce
2 T. hot sauce
1¹/2 tsp. salt

In glass mixing bowl, combine vinegar, lemon juice and garlic and let stand for 2 hours. Combine butter and mustard in medium bowl, stirring until well blended. Add Worcestershire sauce, hot sauce and salt and stir until well blended. Cover and refrigerate overnight to develop proper flavor; can be refrigerated for a few days. Simmer sauce over medium heat for 30 minutes before using.

Kelly Kutz
North St. Petersburg, FL

Marinated Three-Bean Salad

MARINATED THREE-BEAN SALAD

2 (15-oz.) cans dark red kidney
   beans, drained
1 (15-oz.) cans butter beans, drained
3 cups fresh or frozen cut green beans
2 cups sliced celery
1 large onion, sliced
1 medium green or red bell pepper,
   cut into 1-inch pieces

$^3/_4$ cup white vinegar
$^3/_4$ cup vegetable oil
$^3/_4$ cup granulated sugar
2 cloves garlic, minced
$^1/_4$ cup fresh basil, firmly packed
2 tsp. salt
1 tsp. coarsely ground pepper

Combine beans, celery, onion and bell pepper in large bowl. Combine vinegar, oil, sugar, garlic, basil, salt and pepper in a saucepan. Bring to boil. Pour over beans and vegetables and mix. Cover and chill, stirring several times. When ready to serve, drain marinade.

Linda G. Lilley
Farmville, VA

BAKED POTATOES ON THE GRILL

Baking potatoes
$^1/_2$ cup butter
Onion, sliced
Chives, chopped

Garlic, sliced
Broccoli, chopped
Real or imitation bacon bits

Scrub potatoes and make slits with knife. Slice butter and onion and insert 1 piece of each in each potato slit. Can also insert chives, garlic, broccoli, bacon or other favorite seasonings. Wrap each potato tightly in foil and grill for 25 minutes or until soft in the middle, turning halfway through cooking.

Scott Van Meter
Sheffield Lake, OH

Salmon au Poivre

MAIN DISHES

SALMON AU POIVRE
MARINATED SALMON SEARED IN BLACK PEPPER CRUST

³/4 to 1 lb. center cut salmon fillet,
*   skinned and halved*
2 T. soy sauce
1 clove garlic, minced or crushed
2 tsp. fresh lemon juice

1 tsp. sugar
4 tsp. coarsely ground black pepper
2 T. quality olive oil
Fresh parsley
Lemon slices

Combine soy sauce, garlic, lemon and sugar in zip-top plastic bag. Add salmon, coating well, and marinate for 30 minutes, sealed and chilled. Remove salmon from bag and pat dry; discard marinade. Press 2 teaspoons black pepper onto each side of salmon, coating it thoroughly.

Heat oil over medium-high heat in heavy skillet until hot but not smoking. Sauté salmon 3¹/2 to 4 minutes on each side or until it flakes. Transfer salmon with slotted spatula to paper towel and drain for 30 seconds. Squeeze fresh lemon juice over fish and garnish with fresh parsley and a lemon slice. Serve with Chardonnay or Oregon Pinot Gris.

Gene Brown
Raleigh, NC

PORK LOIN WITH RICE

8-lb. pork loin roast
4 cups Italian bread crumbs
2 T. fresh sage, finely chopped
5 cloves garlic, minced
Pepper
1 1/3 cups Dijon mustard
2 large onions, sliced
3 large oranges, sliced
4 cups apple cider
Salt
3 cups rice, cooked

Combine bread crumbs, sage, garlic, and pepper and set aside. Brush meat with 1 cup mustard and roll in bread crumb mixture. Secure onion slices and orange slices to meat with butcher's string. Roast at 350°F until meat is done and juices run clear.

Remove pork from pan. Place pan on medium heat and add apple cider. Boil gently until thickened. Add 1/3 cup Dijon mustard and salt to taste. Strain sauce and serve on the side. Slice pork 1-inch thick and serve with rice, green salad and garlic bread.

Alton E. Mickle
Birmingham, AL

CHEESE FRENCHIES

6 slices bread
6 slices American cheese
Mayonnaise
1 egg, well beaten
1/2 cup milk
1/2 tsp. salt
3/4 cup flour

Make sandwiches of bread, cheese and mayonnaise; cut in quarters. Mix egg, milk, salt and flour to make batter. Dip each quarter in batter to cover, mixing batter after each dip. Coat each quarter with cornflake crumbs. Deep fry. For best results in making cornflakes stick, make sandwiches ahead and freeze before deep frying.

Gladys Jackson
Hershey, NE

SPAM KABOBS

12-oz. can Spam luncheon meat
1 doz. cherry tomatoes
1 large bell pepper
1 large onion
1 medium yellow squash

1 medium zucchini
6 large whole mushrooms
1 can pineapple wedges (optional)
Bamboo skewers

Cut Spam into 24 1-inch cubes. Cut bell pepper and onion into wedges. Slice squash and zucchini into 1-inch pieces. Slice mushrooms in half. Assemble Spam and vegetables on skewers, using 2 vegetables to 1 Spam cube, ending with a tomato or mushroom at the tip to keep other pieces in place. Add pineapple if desired. Marinate in shallow rectangular glass dish for at least 2 hours before cooking. Brush additional sauce on skewers while grilling.

• MARINADE •

1 tsp. liquid smoke flavoring
1 tsp. Worcestershire sauce
1 cup hickory-flavored barbecue sauce
1 T. steak sauce

3 T. honey
2 T. minced garlic
Coarse-ground black pepper

Mix all ingredients in saucepan on medium heat, stirring until well blended.

Anthony Lanting
Hunstville, AL

BARBECUE ON BUNS

1½ lbs. ground beef
1 small onion, diced
1 can tomato soup
½ cup water
½ cup ketchup
2 squirts mustard
1 T. brown sugar
Cheese slices (optional)

Brown ground beef and onion. Add tomato soup, water, ketchup, mustard and brown sugar. Heat through and serve on toasted hamburger buns. Good with cheese slice.

Jill and Joel Ramthun
Litchfield, MN

EVELYN'S SIMPLE BEEF ROAST

4- to 5-lb. beef roast, frozen
2 pkgs. onion soup mix
Aluminum foil

Wash frozen roast and rub with onion soup powder. Wrap in 4 to 5 layers of aluminum foil after pouring remaining soup powder on top of roast. Bake at 250°F for 6 to 8 hours. Remove from wrap, slice and serve. Pour juice over roast or serve as gravy over potatoes.

Guy Claypool
Chaparral, NM

SMOKED TURKEY

1 medium or large turkey
Several cloves garlic, sliced
Italian dressing
2 cans caffeine-free cola
Melted butter

Make 8 to 10 slits in meaty parts of turkey (breast, drumstick, between thigh and chest). Insert garlic slices into slits. Cover turkey with salad dressing. Pour ½ can cola and small quantity of butter into cavity. Place bird in smoker with remaining cola in water pan of smoker. When bird is cooked to desired doneness, pour any remaining salad dressing over bird. Can substitute wine for cola.

William Leistner
Maryville, TN

EASY OVEN-BROWNED STEW

1 lb. boneless beef, cut into 1-inch cubes
$^1/_3$ to $^1/_2$ cup quick-cooking tapioca
3 ribs celery, cut into 1-inch pieces
5 to 6 carrots, cut into 1-inch pieces
2 medium onions, quartered
4 medium potatoes
1 or 2 (16-oz.) cans tomatoes
14-oz. can green beans, with liquid reserved
$^1/_2$ cup water
1 T. salt
$^1/_8$ tsp. pepper
1 T. sugar

Arrange meat in bottom of enamel roaster or large pan. Sprinkle tapioca over meat according to desire thickness of finished stew. Add celery, carrots, onions, potatoes and tomatoes. Combine liquid from beans with water and salt, pepper and sugar. Pour over vegetables and meat. Cover tightly with lid or foil and bake at 300°F for 4 to 4$^1/_2$ hours, or at 250°F for 4$^1/_2$ to 6 hours. Can be cooked overnight in slow cooker set to low. Refrigerate drained beans and stir into stew when stew is done.

Gladys Jackson
Hershey, NE

GRILLED PORK WRAPS

Pork tenderloin or boneless loin chops,
cut 1 to 1$^1/_4$-inch thick
Bacon
Salt and pepper
Onion, sliced about $^3/_8$-inch thick
Tomato, sliced about $^3/_8$-inch thick
Green peppers, quartered
Cheddar cheese, cut into 2 x $^1/_2$-inch pieces
Wooden toothpicks

Place 2 pieces of bacon in an X. Place 1 piece of loin in middle of X. Salt and pepper. Place 1 slice onion, 1 slice tomato and 1 piece green pepper on top of pork. Bring bacon ends up and secure to top of green pepper with toothpick. Grill using indirect method, roasting 40 to 45 minutes directly on grill rack over drip pan. Add coals as necessary to keep grill hot.

When pork is done, place one piece cheddar cheese on each wrap and return wrap to grill until cheese melts. Can prepare wraps early in the day and refrigerate until ready to grill.

Jan Omernik
Stevens Point, WI

BESSIE HANAHAN'S CRAB CAKES

1 lb. fresh crab meat, well picked over
1 lemon
4 T. unsalted butter
2 T. finely chopped Vidalia or
    other sweet onion
$^1/_2$ cup chopped ripened bell pepper
    (or $^1/_4$ cup green)
1 T. sherry vinegar
1 large egg, beaten

Salt
Freshly ground black pepper
Seasoned salt
Cayenne pepper (optional)
Fresh herbs (optional)
Hot sauce (optional)
Worcestershire sauce (optional)
2 to 3 T. clarified butter
Fine dry bread crumbs

Sprinkle crab meat with juice of $^1/_2$ lemon to freshen it. If lemon isn't juicy, use whole lemon. Melt butter in heavy skillet over low heat and add onion and bell pepper, cooking until onion becomes transparent. Add vinegar, increase heat and cook until vinegar has evaporated. Pour the mixture over crab meat, add egg and toss, being careful not to break larger clumps of crab meat. Season to taste with salt, pepper, cayenne pepper, fresh herbs, hot sauce and/or Worcestershire sauce. Refrigerate for several hours or freeze for 15 minutes.

Place clarified butter in skillet over medium heat. Form crab cake mixture into 3 large or 6 small patties. Roll patties in bread crumbs and fry in butter for 3 to 4 minutes over medium heat until golden brown. Handle very, very carefully to keep them intact until they reach serving plate, but don't worry if they break. Serve with a spicy green mayonnaise on a bed of fresh lettuce with vine-ripened tomatoes. Or serve with garlic toast: Toast day-old French bread slices and rub with garlic and good olive oil, then top with tomato slices, salt, pepper and fresh basil.

Gene Brown
Raleigh, NC

Bessie Hanahan's Crab Cakes

CABINET DOOR SPICE RACK

Guy Claypool of Chaparral, New Mexico, designed this spice rack to be attached to the back of a cabinet door. It is a simple project to build: the ends of the rack are cut from dimensional pine to 3 × 5", then a $1^3/_4 \times 1^3/_4$" cutout is made at the top front corner of each part. The bottom of the rack is also cut from dimensional pine. It butts up to the inside edges of the ends and is fastened with glue and finish nails.

A center shelf made from $^1/_4$" plywood can be adjusted according to the height of the spice containers stored on the bottom of the rack (the $2^1/_4$" spec shown here allows clearance for standard spice cans). Dowels ($^1/_4$" dia.) are inserted between the ends to make guard railings that keep the containers from falling out.

A $^1/_4$" plywood pack panel is attached to the ends and bottom, flush with the outside edges. Attach the back panel to the door with #6 × $^3/_4$" wood screws. Make sure there is a 2-in. wide border around the sides and bottom of the spice rack.

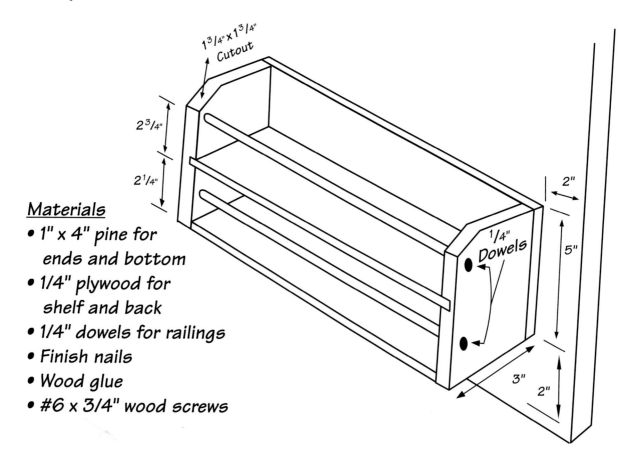

Materials
- 1" x 4" pine for ends and bottom
- 1/4" plywood for shelf and back
- 1/4" dowels for railings
- Finish nails
- Wood glue
- #6 x 3/4" wood screws

LINGUINE WITH WHITE CLAM SAUCE

8 oz. linguine
3 T. olive oil
1 large onion, chopped
6 cloves garlic, chopped
2 T. flour
6^{1}/2-oz. can minced clams, juice reserved
^{1}/4 cup clam juice
1 cup chicken broth
^{1}/4 cup grated Parmesan cheese
2 T. minced parsley

Cook linguine according to package directions, omitting the salt. Rinse with cold water, drain and set aside. Meanwhile, in heavy 10-inch skillet, heat olive oil for 1 minute over medium heat. Sauté onion and garlic about 5 minutes, until onion is soft. Blend in flour and cook, stirring constantly, for 1 minute. Add clams, clam juice and chicken broth; cook and stir for 4 minutes. Add cooked linguine and cook for 1 minute, tossing well until heated through. Mix in parsley, sprinkle with Parmesan cheese and serve.

Fran Goran
Gowanda, NY

SPAM-A-RONI & CHEESE

1 box macaroni and cheese
2 T. minced garlic
7-oz. can Spam luncheon meat
1 small onion
4-oz. can sliced mushrooms
^{1}/2 cup frozen peas
Salt and pepper

Prepare macaroni and cheese according to package directions, adding garlic to boiling water. Dice Spam and onion into ^{1}/4-inch cubes. Add Spam, onion and mushrooms to macaroni and cheese. Stir on low heat until well mixed. Add peas and season to taste with salt and pepper. Cover and cook for 2 minutes before serving.

Anthony Lanting
Hunstville, AL

JOEL'S HAMBURGERS

1¹/₂ lbs. ground beef
1 egg
1 packet onion soup mix
20 soda crackers, crushed
Salt and pepper

Combine beef, egg, soup mix, crackers, salt and pepper. Form into hamburger patties. Grill and serve on toasted hamburger buns.

Jill and Joel Ramthun
Litchfield, MN

CRAB SALAD

1 pkg. imitation crab meat	1 rib celery, finely
4 oz. sour cream	chopped
3 heaping T. mayonnaise	10-oz. pkg. fine egg
1 cucumber, peeled,	noodles, cooked
seeded and diced	Dash salt and pepper

Shred crab meat with fork. Mix sour cream, mayonnaise, cucumber, celery, noodles, salt and pepper into crab meat. Add more or less sour cream and mayonnaise to taste.

Lesa and Mark Kilpatrick
Warren, AR

TOMATO BEEF SAUCE

2 lbs. chuck steak, cut into bite-size pieces
15-oz. can Mexican-style stewed tomatoes
15-oz. can Italian-style stewed tomatoes
15-oz. can thick, zesty tomato sauce
2¹/₂ cups water
1 to 3 cubes beef bouillon
1 cup lentils
1 medium onion, chopped
1 scant T. butter
Garlic (optional)
Salt (optional)
Pepper, plain or seasoned (optional)

Brown chuck steak pieces in oil in a large pot. Add stewed tomatoes, tomato sauce, water, bouillon, lentils, onion, butter and garlic, salt and pepper, if desired; stir thoroughly and bring to a boil. Lower heat and simmer for 1 hour, stirring occasionally. Uncover and cook to desired consistency. Serve over rice or pasta.

Leslie Sanderfer
Baytown, TX

VENISON STEW

4 to 6 lbs. venison, cut into cubes
Salt and pepper
1 cup flour
$^1/_4$ cup hot bacon drippings or hot fat
2 large onions, coarsely chopped
1 large can tomato juice
$^1/_2$ tsp. garlic powder
1 bay leaf
1 T. Worcestershire sauce
1 bay leaf

1 tsp. leaf oregano
1 tsp. ground thyme
1 tsp. ground cumin
1 T. basil leaves
$^1/_2$ tsp. salt
1 tsp. pepper
6 to 8 white potatoes, peeled and cubed
3 large carrots, cut into $^1/_2$-inch pieces
$^1/_4$ cups chopped celery

Salt and pepper meat and dredge in flour. Braise meat in hot bacon drippings or fat. Transfer to large pot and add onions, tomato juice, garlic powder, bay leaf, Worcestershire sauce, oregano, thyme, cumin, basil, salt and pepper. Cover and simmer for 2 to 2$^1/_2$ hours or until meat is tender, stirring occasionally. Add potatoes, carrots and celery; continue cooking 30 to 45 minutes or until vegetables are tender. Remove bay leaf.

Robert L. Rutherford
Russiaville, IN

Cousin Jack's Pasties

COUSIN JACK'S PASTIES

1 to 2 lbs. beef, ground or cubed
3 cups flour
1 tsp. salt
3/4 cup lard
1/2 cup water
4 small potatoes, peeled and cubed
2 rutabagas, peeled and cubed
2 carrots, diced
1 onion, diced
1 small cabbage, diced
Salt and pepper
1 T. cream of mushroom soup (optional)
1 egg, beaten (optional)
Butter (optional)

Brown and drain meat; set aside. Combine flour with salt and cut in lard until it forms coarsely flaked dough. Sprinkle dough with water, adding as little as possible to work dough into ball. Divide ball into 6 portions. Roll each ball on lightly floured surface into a 6- to 9-inch circle. Lay each circle of dough in a 6- to 9-inch pie pan.

Combine meat and all vegetables and season to taste with salt and pepper. If desired, add 1 tablespoon cream of mushroom soup for flavor and moistener. Place about 1 cup of mixture in center of each round. Fold over and brush with beaten egg or butter. Bake at 450°F for 45 minutes.

John Tengelitsch
Buchanan, MI

SWEET AND SOUR LITTLE ONIONS WITH SAUSAGES EUGENE

2 (16-oz.) or 3 (10-oz.) pkgs. frozen
pearl onions, thawed
1/4 cup butter
1/4 cup dark brown sugar
1/4 cup red wine vinegar
Salt
3/4 to 1 lb. hot Italian sausage (optional)
Extra virgin olive oil

Drain onions well on paper towels. Melt butter in large heavy skillet (or 2 smaller ones). When butter foams, add onions and sauté over medium-high heat for 5 to 8 minutes or until onions begin to color. Add brown sugar and stir to coat onions. Add vinegar and salt and cook 2 to 3 minutes. Transfer to warmed serving dish and serve hot.

If including sausage, skin hot Italian sausage of its casings and cut into 1/2-inch rounds. Brown sausage pieces in olive oil in pan used for onions. Drain briefly and add to onions. Serve hot.

Gene Brown
Raleigh, NC

RANDY'S QUICK CONCOCTION

7-oz. box chicken-flavored rice
24-oz. can fat-free chicken and dumplings
15-oz. can mixed vegetables
10-oz. can cream of chicken soup

Prepare rice according to package directions. Open all three cans; drain half of juice from chicken and dumplings and all juice from vegetables. Mix all ingredients with rice and microwave for 4 to 5 minutes.

Randy Goodwin
Columbia, TN

SLOW-COOK LASAGNA

2 lbs. ground beef
1 large onion, chopped
7-oz. can chopped mushrooms
1-lb. box lasagna noodles
3 (27 1/2-oz.) jars chunky garden-style spaghetti sauce
3 (8-oz.) bags shredded colby and Monterey Jack cheese blend

Brown ground beef with onion and mushrooms. Cook noodles according to package directions until about half done. Add spaghetti sauce to ground beef mixture to make filling. In 6-quart slow cooker, layer filling, noodles and cheese, ending with cheese. Cook for about 2 hours on high.

Nancy Colwell
Decatur, IN

OPENING UP A KITCHEN & DINING ROOM

Though this kitchen was perfectly functional, the series of balusters extending upward from the stub walls created a "caged-in" feeling. So Jan Omernik of Steven's Point, Wisconsin, improved the ambience by doing away with the balusters and changing the flooring and window treatments for a more open feeling.

Before

Before

TURKEY IN A BAG

Turkey
Butter, softened

Favorite poultry seasonings
Paper grocery sack

Clean and dry turkey and rub skin with softened butter. Sprinkle with desired seasonings. Place turkey in paper grocery sack, close bag, roll end one or twice and staple. Place on rack in roasting pan. Roast, uncovered, at 325° for about 20 minutes per pound until internal temperature reaches 180°F to 185°. Remove turkey from oven, pierce bag to allow juices to run into pan for gravy if desired. Remove turkey from bag and carve.

Michael Herrick
Golden, CO

TERIYAKI CHICKEN

Chicken
$1^{1}/_{4}$ cups soy sauce
$1/_{4}$ cup salad oil
$3/_{4}$ cup pineapple juice
1 cup water
$1^{1}/_{2}$ T. lemon juice

2 T. vinegar
$3/_{4}$ tsp. dry garlic
$1^{1}/_{2}$ tsp. ground ginger
$1/_{2}$ cup brown sugar
$1/_{4}$ cup finely chopped onion
Pineapple slices (optional)

Combine soy sauce, salad oil, pineapple juice, water, lemon juice and vinegar. In a separate bowl, mix garlic, ginger, sugar and onion; add to liquid, stirring well. Refrigerate chicken in marinade for at least 3 hours before grilling. Grill pineapple slices if desired and place on grilled chicken.

George Olsson
Orlando, FL

Turkey in a Bag

JIM'S SWISS CHICKEN BAKE

2 lbs. skinless, boneless chicken breasts, cut into pieces
1/4 cup butter
6-oz. pkg stuffing mix
10 1/2-oz. can cream of mushroom soup
10 1/2-oz. can cream of celery soup
6 T. water
Pinch thyme
1/8 tsp. granulated garlic
1/2 tsp. poultry seasoning
1/2 tsp. salt
1/2 tsp. pepper
1 1/2 lbs. sliced Swiss cheese
Cooking spray

Sauté chicken pieces in butter over medium heat until about half done. Spray 9 x 13-inch baking pan with cooking spray. Transfer chicken and butter to pan.

Mix stuffing mix, soups, water, thyme, garlic, poultry seasoning, salt and pepper in mixing bowl. Arrange cheese slices over chicken, then layer stuffing mix. Repeat. Bake, uncovered, at 375°F for 40 to 60 minutes or until golden brown.

James Mullen
East Meredith, NY

CAMP STEW

1 chicken fryer or hen
1 lb. beef
1 lb. lean pork, cut up
2 (14 1/2-oz.) cans peeled, whole tomatoes
2 (14 3/4-oz.) cans cream corn
2 (15-oz.) cans mixed vegetables
2 lbs. onion, chopped
Ketchup
Worcestershire sauce
Hot sauce
Salt
Pepper
1/2 cup sugar
Lemon juice
Lemon rind

Boil meats in very large covered pot or pressure cooker until meat falls apart. Remove all bones. Add tomatoes, corn, vegetables and onion and cook slowly for 15 minutes, stirring constantly to prevent sticking. Add ketchup, Worcestershire sauce, hot sauce, salt and pepper to taste and stir. Add sugar, lemon juice and rind to taste. Cook very slowly for about 2 hours. Serve with bread or rice and dill pickles.

Charles D. Segrest
Auburn, AL

ONE-DISH MEATLOAF MEAL

1 lb. ground beef or ground turkey
^{1}/2 cup bread cube stuffing
^{1}/4 cup milk
1 egg
^{1}/4 tsp. salt
10^3/4-oz. can cream of celery soup
Frozen ready-to-eat potato bits

Mix ground meat with bread stuffing, milk, egg and salt and pat into baking dish. Cover meatloaf with cream of celery soup. Top with potato bits, spaced about 1 inch apart. Bake at 300°F for 1 hour or microwave on high for 30 minutes.

J.R. Hackenberry
Summerville, PA

SHRIMP ETOUFFÉE

2 lbs. fresh or frozen medium shrimp,
peeled and deveined
1^1/2-oz. shrimp or crab boil
1 cup butter or margarine
1 large white onion, chopped
3 bundles green onions, sliced ^{1}/4-inch thick
3 T. chopped garlic
Black pepper
Red pepper
1 tsp. oregano
16 oz. tomato sauce
4 (10^1/2-oz.) cans cream of chicken soup
10^1/2-oz. can cream of shrimp soup
2 T. Worcestershire sauce
Steamed white rice

Cook shrimp in shrimp or crab boil. Melt butter in large skillet over low heat. Add white onion, green onion, garlic, red and black pepper and oregano. Simmer until white onion is translucent. Add tomato sauce, soup and Worcestershire. Cook over medium heat for about 15 minutes, stirring often. Add shrimp and cook long enough to warm shrimp. Serve in bowls, ladling etouffée over scoops of fluffy rice.

Kathy Hart
Spring, TX

KITCHEN ISLAND PULL-OUT TABLE

One side of this kitchen island has blind drawer and doors. The middle drawer pulls out for napkins, and the table pulls out as shown. The other side has three doors and the two outside drawers will open.

The entire cabinet is covered with plastic laminate counter stock.

Edwin Buckta
Jasper, IN

SLOPPY JOES

1½ lbs. ground beef
½ cup chopped green pepper
½ cup chopped onion
2 cloves garlic, minced
16-oz. can tomato sauce
½ cup ketchup
2 tsp. brown sugar
2½ tsp. prepared mustard
1 T. Worcestershire
1 T. chili powder (or to taste)
Cheddar cheese (optional)

Cook ground beef, green pepper, onion and garlic in large skillet until vegetables are tender and meat is browned. Stir in tomato sauce, ketchup, brown sugar, mustard, Worcestershire sauce and chili powder. Cover and simmer 15 minutes. Serve on buns, topped with cheddar cheese.

Kenny Campbell
Lawrenceburg, KY

MARK'S SPAGHETTI SAUCE

1 lb. ground beef or
  ground turkey
2 (6-oz.) cans tomato paste
3 cups water
2 T. dried minced onion
  (or fresh)

1 tsp. garlic salt
⅛ tsp. black pepper
4-oz. can mushrooms
Spaghetti, cooked according
  to package instructions

Brown ground meat and drain. Add tomato paste, water, onion, garlic salt, pepper and mushrooms. Cover and simmer 20 minutes, stirring occasionally. Serve over hot spaghetti.

Mark Stone
Antioch, CA

EASY BARBECUE PORK RIBS

6 country-style pork ribs
48-oz. can pineapple juice
Bottle favorite barbecue sauce

Trim excess fat from ribs. Boil ribs with juice in large pot for about 45 minutes. Drain juice and baste with sauce. Broil or grill for 1½ to 2 minutes on each side. Baste again and let stand for 5 minutes before serving.

Jim Bray
Fresno, CA

TURKEY WITH INJECTED MARINADE

1 turkey
1 cup butter or margarine
1¹/2 cups lemon juice
2 tsp. salt
1 T. liquid garlic
25 to 30 drops hot sauce

Melt butter and add lemon juice, salt, liquid garlic and hot sauce. While hot, inject by needle into turkey or other meat. Makes enough for a 14-pound turkey. Roast turkey as usual.

Ken Goerdt
Hibbing, MN

POP'S SLUMGULLION

2 onions, diced
2 T. cooking oil
2 (15-oz.) cans corned beef
2 (15-oz.) cans peas, drained
2 (15-oz.) cans corn, drained
2 (14-oz.) cans tomato sauce

Sauté onions in oil in large cast iron skillet. Add corned beef, peas and corn. Stir in tomato sauce and cook for 15 minutes, stirring occasionally.

Guy and Evelyn Claypool
Chapparal, NM

SPAGHETTI WITH MUSSELS, SCALLOPS AND SHRIMP

3 T. light olive oil
1 large onion, minced
2 to 3 cloves garlic, minced
¹/4 cup dry white wine
1¹/2 tsp. dried basil or 1¹/2 T. fresh
1 tsp. dried marjoram or 1T. fresh
10-oz. can crushed tomatoes, well drained
6-oz. can tomato paste
1 lb. mussels, scrubbed and debearded
1¹/2 to 2 lbs. small clams, scrubbed
1 lb. sea scallops, halved
1 lb. (20 to 30 pieces) cooked shrimp at room temperature
1 lb. spaghetti, cooked al denté

Heat oil in large saucepan over medium-high heat. Add onion and sauté until lightly golden. Add garlic and sauté 30 seconds. Stir in wine, basil and marjoram and cook 1 minute. Add tomatoes and increase heat; boil 5 minutes. Reduce heat to medium, add mussels and clams, cover and cook about 5 minutes or until shells open about ¹/2 inch. Add scallops and cook 2 to 3 minutes or until barely firm. Add cooked shrimp and cook 1 minute, just until warm. Add spaghetti and toss gently to mix.

Larry Stoloff
Sharon, MA

Kitchen cabinet hideaway drawer

William F. Jones Sr. of Binghamton, New York, sent this clever tip that takes advantage of unused space beneath your base cabinets to create a secret hiding place. He simply cut out a section of the cabinet toe-kick and used it as a drawer front. By tacking ell-shaped cleats to the underside of the cabinet as shown in the illustration, he provided surfaces for attaching drawer slides, as well as nailing surfaces for the cut ends of the toe kick. A magnetic door catch mounted near the toe kick area of the cabinet works with a metal channel on the drawer front to make sure the drawer stays shut.

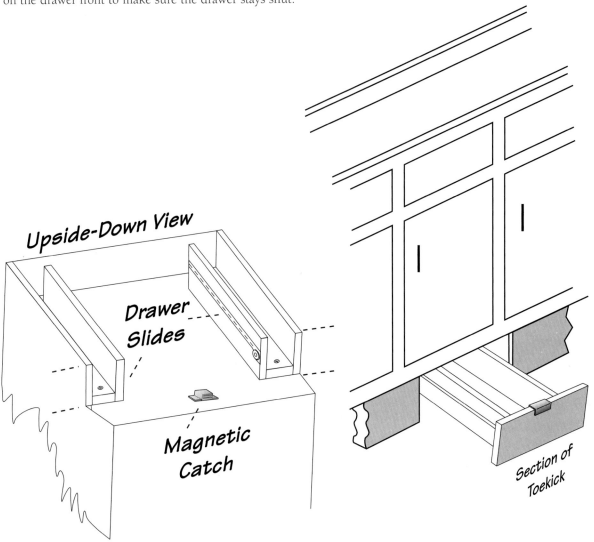

Upside-Down View

Drawer Slides

Magnetic Catch

Section of Toekick

Chicken Tetrazzini

CHICKEN TETRAZZINI

3 cups chicken, cooked and cubed

8 oz. spaghetti

1 medium onion, chopped

5 T. butter

4-oz. can mushrooms, drained

3 T. all-purpose flour

2 cups chicken stock or broth

$^3/_4$ cup Parmesan cheese

1 T. parsley

$^1/_8$ tsp. savory

1 tsp. salt

$^1/_8$ tsp. black pepper

$^3/_4$ cup milk

3 T. dry vermouth or white wine

Cook spaghetti and chop into pieces. Sauté onion in 1 tablespoon butter; add mushrooms. Heat 4 tablespoons butter on medium heat until it bubbles, then add flour to make paste. Add broth, stirring constantly. Add half of cheese and the parsley, savory, salt and pepper and stir until thick and creamy. Add milk and vermouth, stir and continue to cook until thick.

Combine spaghetti, onion, mushrooms and chicken with thickened mixture in baking dish and stir. Sprinkle with remaining cheese. Bake, uncovered, at 375°F for 20 minutes.

Ronald L. Fox
Louisville, KY

BARBECUE PIZZA

1 lb. lean ground beef

$^1/_2$ cup onion, minced

$^3/_4$ cup corn

$^3/_4$ cup barbecue sauce

$^1/_2$ tsp. salt

1 large pizza shell

8 oz. cheddar cheese, grated

Brown ground beef and drain. Add onion, corn, barbecue sauce and salt and heat through. Place pizza shell on baking sheet. Top with beef mixture and sprinkle with cheese. Bake at 425°F for 12 to 15 minutes or until cheese melts.

Kevin J. Dirth
Muscatine, IA

EVELYN'S LASAGNA

8 oz. lean ground meat
28-oz. jar pasta sauce
1 lb. pkg. lasagna noodles
Any combination of mozzarella, cheddar,
Monterey Jack, provolone,
cottage or Ricotta cheese

Cook noodles if desired. Brown meat and drain. Place small amount of sauce in bottom of large baking pan. Cover bottom of pan with 4 noodles; add cheese and more sauce, then 4 noodles. Add layer of meat, sauce and cheese, then 4 noodles, sauce and cheese. Bake at 400°F for 20 to 25 minutes.

Guy Claypool
Chapparal, NM

SANDERFER BEEF STEW

1¹/₂-lb. can beef stew
15-oz. can ranch-style
  beans
14¹/₂-oz. can Cajun-style
  or stewed tomatoes

Seasoned pepper mix
Salt
MSG (optional)
Creole seasoning
  (optional)

Mix stew, beans and tomatoes, seasoning to taste. Bring to boil then reduce heat; simmer 20 minutes. Serve over rice or eat as is.

Leslie Sanderfer
Baytown, TX

CHICKEN BAKE

2 to 3 boneless, skinless chicken breast halves
1¹/₂ cups water
¹/₄ cup butter or margarine
6-oz. pkg. stuffing mix for poultry
Favorite chicken seasoning
Greek, Italian, mesquite or herb seasoning (optional)

Heat water and butter in small saucepan until butter is melted. Add stuffing mix and stir until liquid is absorbed. Coat 8 x 8 x 2-inch baking dish with nonstick cooking spray. Spread a thin layer of moistened stuffing mix to completely cover bottom. Place chicken breasts in baking dish and sprinkle with desired seasonings. Add remaining stuffing mix in thin layer over chicken.

Cover with aluminum foil and bake at 325°F for 45 minutes. Remove foil and continue baking for 15 minutes. Serve hot.

Steve Ball
Golden Valley, AZ

BEEF STROGANOFF

$1^1/_2$ lbs. beef fillet
4 T. butter or margarine
1 large yellow onion, peeled and diced
$^1/_2$ lb. fresh mushrooms
   or 6-oz. can sliced mushrooms
1 tsp. meat glaze
1 tsp. tomato paste
2 T. flour

1 cup stock or bouillon
$1^1/_2$ tsp. salt
1 tsp. pepper
1 cup sour cream
1 tsp. sugar
1 T. fruit brandy
2 tsp. finely cut dill

Trim fat and sinew from beef; cut meat against grain into 2-inch strips $^1/_2$-inch thick. Brown in 2 tablespoons butter in heavy stoveproof casserole. Melt 2 tablespoons butter in small skillet; cook onion and mushrooms over moderate heat until onion is tender but not brown. Remove skillet from heat and stir in glaze and tomato paste. Mix flour smoothly with small amount of stock or bouillon and stir into mixture. Gradually add remaining stock or bouillon.

Return pan to heat and stir until sauce begins to boil. Add salt and pepper. Add sour cream in small amounts, stirring into center of sauce and stirring steadily. Stir in sugar and fruit brandy. Pour over beef in casserole and sprinkle with 1 teaspoon dill. Cover and bake at 375°F for 20 minutes or until heated through. Extend cooking time 25 to 30 minutes if using a less tender cut of beef. Sprinkle with remaining teaspoon dill. Serve with noodles.

Charles D. Segrest
Auburn, AL

WHACK'S CHILI

4 lbs. lean beef chuck or venison
Oil
Meat tenderizer
1 large onion, diced
1 large green pepper, diced
4 whole hot red peppers, diced
2 large ribs celery, diced
2 cloves garlic, minced
14^1/2-oz. can diced tomatoes
7^1/2 oz. can tomato sauce
4 oz. can tomato paste

2 (12-oz.) cans hot chili beans
8 T. chili powder
1 T. ground cumin
^{1}/2 tsp. cayenne pepper
Hot sauce
6 oz. beer (optional)
2 bay leaves
Garlic salt
Salt and pepper
Water
Shredded cheddar or colby cheese

Cut meat into bite-size pieces and brown in oil in large skillet as room allows. Drain off grease and transfer meat to large cooking pot. Sprinkle with meat tenderizer. Sauté onion, green pepper, red peppers, celery and garlic in same skillet, and transfer to cooking pot with meat. Add tomatoes, tomato sauce, tomato paste, chili beans, chili powder, cumin, cayenne pepper, hot sauce, beer, bay leaves, garlic salt and salt and pepper to taste. Add just enough water to cover ingredients. Cover pot with lid and cook on low heat for 3 hours, stirring often.

Remove bay leaves. Serve with shredded cheese and oyster crackers.

John "Whack" Czarneski
Sunman, IN

CRAZY CRUST PIZZA

1¹/₂ lbs. ground beef or sausage
or 1 cup thinly sliced pepperoni
1 cup flour
1 T. pizza or Italian seasoning
2 eggs
²/₃ cup milk
Onion, chopped (optional)
Green pepper, chopped (optional)
4-oz. can mushroom stems and pieces,
drained (optional)
Other favorite toppings
15-oz. jar spaghetti sauce
2 cups shredded mozzarella cheese

Brown ground beef in medium skillet; drain and set aside. Lightly grease 12- or 14-inch pizza pan or 15¹/₂ x 10¹/₂ x 1-inch jellyroll pan. Mix flour, seasoning, eggs and milk and pour into pan, tilting pan to completely cover bottom. Arrange meat and toppings of your choice. Bake on low oven rack at 375°F for 20 to 30 minutes until crust is lightly browned. Remove from oven, spread sauce over pizza and sprinkle with cheese. Bake for an additional 10 to 15 minutes or until cheese is melted.

Kurt Schlatter
Bayard, IA

TACO SALAD

1 lb. ground beef
2 pkgs. taco seasoning
1 cup water
8-oz. tub sour cream
1 head lettuce, shredded
2 tomatoes, chopped
1 bunch green onions, chopped
1 can sliced black olives
8 oz. colby cheese, grated
Guacamole to garnish
Salsa to garnish

Brown ground beef; add 1 package taco seasoning and water. Simmer until meat is cooked. Mix sour cream and 2nd package of taco seasoning. Spread seasoned sour cream evenly over large platter. Spread taco meat over sour cream. Layer with lettuce, tomatoes, green onions and black olives. Smother with cheese and top with guacamole and salsa. Refrigerate for 1 to 2 hours. Serve with tortilla chips.

Lesa and Mark Kilpatrick
Warren, AR

ERIC'S GRANDE BURRITOS

4 skinless, boneless chicken breasts, diced
1 large onion, diced
4 oz. black olives, diced
15-oz. can Mexican-style stewed tomatoes
1 cup salsa
1 can refried beans
8 10- to 12-inch flour tortillas
8 oz. shredded mozzarella cheese
8 oz. shredded cheddar cheese
Lettuce
Sour cream

Brown chicken and onion in skillet over high heat. When chicken is cooked, add olives, stewed tomatoes and salsa. Cook refried beans on low heat.

Place tortillas on cookie sheet and place one scoop each refried beans and chicken mixture onto each tortilla shell. Top with generous amount of cheese. Fold over and bake at 350°F for 10 to 15 minutes. Serve over bed of lettuce with sour cream.

Eric Cotton
Tampa, FL

STIR-FRIED PORK & VEGETABLES

1 lb. pork, cut across the grain
into $1/8$-inch strips
2 T. soy sauce
$2^1/2$ tsp. cornstarch
$1^1/2$ tsp. sugar
$1/4$ tsp. ginger
3 tsp. oil
8-oz. pkg. frozen broccoli
4-oz. can mushroom pieces
1 carrot, thinly sliced
$1/2$ cup chopped onion
$1/4$ tsp. salt

Mix pork with soy sauce, cornstarch, sugar and ginger. Heat $1^1/2$ teaspoons oil in wok or skillet and add broccoli, mushrooms, mushroom liquid, carrot, onion and salt. Stir-fry until tender crisp. Transfer to warm bowl.

Heat $1^1/2$ teaspoons oil in same pan, and cook pork until browned, about 5 minutes, stirring constantly. Add vegetables to pork, heat through and serve with rice.

Hilda Hoffmann
Preston, MN

CHICKEN & SPINACH RAVIOLI

3 cups semolina or unbleached
   all-purpose flour
1 tsp. salt
4 large eggs, beaten

1 T. olive oil
2 to 3 T. water
Chicken and spinach filling
   (recipe below)

Sift flour and salt; add eggs, olive oil and water and shape into ball. Knead for 10 minutes until dough becomes smooth. Add flour or water as needed. Place dough in plastic wrap and allow to rest for 1 hour. When ready to use, cut ball into 4 sections and return 3 to plastic wrap. Roll remaining section as thin as possible on floured surface. Place 1 teaspoon chicken and spinach filling 2 inches apart on one side of dough; fold other side over filling and pinch closed. Cut into squares with fluted pastry cutter or pizza wheel. Cook ravioli in hard boiling salted water for 6 to 8 minutes. If placing ravioli in freezer bags, flour each to prevent sticking to others.

• CHICKEN & SPINACH FILLING •

8 oz. boneless skinless chicken
4 T. butter
1/2 tsp. Italian seasoning
1 T. fresh thyme or 1 tsp. dried thyme
Light pinch of salt
Light pinch of pepper

1 small onion, finely chopped
2 T. cooking sherry or white wine
1/2 cup cooked spinach
1 egg
1/3 cup half and half
1/2 tsp. nutmeg

Cut chicken into 1-inch pieces. Melt butter in medium skillet and add Italian seasoning, thyme, salt and pepper and chicken. Sauté for 4 minutes. Add chopped onion and cook until soft, about 2 minutes. Add sherry and cook one more minute. Transfer from skillet to food processor. Place fresh leaf spinach in skillet and cook on low heat until wilted. (If using frozen spinach, remove as much water as possible.) Place spinach in food processor with chicken and pulse until chicken is chopped. Transfer to medium bowl and add egg, half and half and nutmeg. Mix well.

Gary Mallon
Post Falls, ID

GRILLED VEGETABLE & CHICKEN SANDWICH

6 to 8 boneless chicken breasts
¹/₂ cup soy sauce
2 T. olive oil
1 clove garlic, minced
Salt and pepper
2 to 3 green onions, chopped

1 or 2 red peppers, sliced
6 to 8 slices eggplant
6 to 8 slices onion
6 to 8 sandwich rolls
6 to 8 slices feta cheese

For marinade, mix soy sauce, olive oil, garlic, salt, pepper and green onions. Add red pepper, eggplant and onion slices with chicken to marinade; refrigerate for 2 hours. Grill vegetables and chicken to desired doneness. Build sandwich by layering vegetables and chicken on sandwich rolls. Top with a slice of feta or your favorite cheese.

Paul Caruolo
Cary, NC

PIZZA CASSEROLE

2 cups cooked macaroni
1 lb. ground beef
1 onion, finely chopped
10¹/₄-oz. can pizza sauce
15-oz. can spaghetti sauce
³/₄ lb. or more mozzarella cheese, grated

Garlic
Salt
Pepper
Oregano
Pepperoni, sliced

Cook macaroni according to package directions; meanwhile, brown ground beef with onion, salt and pepper. When done, mix macaroni and ground beef. Add sauces and season to taste. Pour half of mixture in large casserole and top with portion of mozzarella cheese. Add remaining mixture and top with pepperoni and remaining cheese. Bake at 350°F for 60 minutes or less.

James Cornell
Bedford, PA

Grilled Vegetable & Chicken Sandwich

PUERTO RICAN PORK ROAST

3- to 4-lb. boneless pork roast
1 T. Worcestershire sauce
2 tsp. hot sauce
Salt and pepper
1 cup water
Fresh garlic cloves, slivered
Dry Italian pepperoni, sliced and quartered
Stuffed green olives

Mix Worcestershire sauce and hot sauce. Salt and pepper roast and rub with sauce mix. Place roast in roasting pan with 1 cup water. Cover and bake at 350°F for 20 minutes. Remove roast from pan and place on cutting board. Using small boning or paring knife, cut 1-inch deep slits in roast. Place a piece of garlic, pepperoni and 1 olive in each opening. Repeat at 1-inch intervals until roast is covered. Return roast to roasting pan and bake until meat is done. Make gravy from juices.

Donald E. Struble
Klamath Falls, OR

BARBECUED MEATBALLS

2 lbs. ground beef or ground venison
2 eggs, beaten
2 cups quick rolled oats
13-oz. can evaporated milk
1 onion, chopped
2 tsp. salt
$^1/_2$ tsp. pepper
$^1/_2$ tsp. garlic powder
2 tsp. chili powder

• SAUCE •

2 cups ketchup
1$^1/_2$ cups brown sugar
$^1/_2$ tsp. garlic powder
$^1/_2$ cup chopped onion

Mix ground meat, eggs, oats, milk, onion, salt, peppers and garlic and chili powders thoroughly. Shape into balls and place in single layer in 9 x 13-inch pan. Bake at 350°F for 1 to 1$^1/_2$ hours. Makes 15 large or 50 small meatballs.

For sauce, mix ketchup, brown sugar, garlic powder and onion. Pour over meatballs in pan.

Gladys Jackson
Hershey, NE

PORK ROAST WITH STRING BEANS AND DUMPLINGS

³/₄-lb. pork loin
Onion
2 T. flour
Water

Garlic
Salt and pepper
2 to 3 quarts string beans

Brown meat in oil; set aside. Brown onion and flour. Add small amount of water and garlic, salt and pepper. Cook for about 30 minutes. Add beans and cook for 2 hours or until meat is nearly done. Make dumplings (below) and let cook about 15 minutes with meat and beans.

• DUMPLINGS •

4 cups flour
1 tsp. salt
¹/₂ tsp. baking powder

4 eggs
1¹/₂ cups milk

Mix flour, salt and baking powder. Add eggs and milk and stir into thick batter. Drop by teaspoon into hot greased skillet and brown on both sides. Add to Pork and String Beans and cook about 15 minutes.

John J. Tengelitsch
Buchanan, MI

OVERHEAD KITCHEN RACKS

Everyone wishes they had more and better kitchen storage space. It's just a fact of life, and it's true no matter how big or small your kitchen is! Rick Emter of Olympia, Washington, developed a unique solution to this age-old problem.

Utilizing a pantry rack, conduit, oak trim and hooks, he created these handy and handsome storage spots for his kitchen: a hanging pan rack and a pot-and-spice rack. Use appropriate stain and paint to match these racks to the kitchen décor, and your kitchen can look as neat and attractive—and be as functional—as Rick's.

Hanging Pan Rack (right) made from oak and dowel pins with hooks to hold the pans.

Pot and spice racks made from a pantry rack, oak-trim pieces, conduit and hooks, then painted to your kitchen color. An oak cupboard door attached to the ceiling over the rack area matches the existing doors.

BURKS-STYLE CHILI

5 lbs. ground beef
2 medium onions, chopped
6 ribs celery, chopped
1 bell pepper, chopped
6 T. chili powder
1 T. paprika
1 T. black pepper
1 T. cumin
1 T. MSG (optional)
1 T. seasoned salt

1 T. sugar
1 tsp. garlic powder
1 tsp. thyme
1 cup water
1 tsp. crushed red peppers
2 (29-oz.) cans tomatoes
29-oz. can tomato puree
1 qt. water
10 cans favorite chili beans (optional)

Sauté onion, celery and bell pepper. Add ground beef and cook until done. Mix chili powder, paprika, black pepper, cumin, MSG, seasoned salt, sugar, garlic powder and thyme in small bowl with 1 cup water. Add seasonings to vegetables and meat and simmer for 30 minutes. Add tomatoes, tomato puree and water and continue cooking several hours or until cooked to desired flavor.

Variations: Serve in place of spaghetti sauce on cooked spaghetti, or serve over hamburger patty, garnished with diced onion and cheese.

Elic H. Burks Jr.
St. Joseph, MO

Charlie's Favorite Chili

CHARLIE'S FAVORITE CHILI

4 lbs. ground beef
1 1/2 medium onions, chopped
1 medium green pepper, chopped
2 jalapeño peppers, chopped
1 small clove garlic, minced
2 T. cooking oil
8 T. chili powder
1 T. cumin

2 tsp. garlic salt
1 can beer
1 T. hot sauce
8-oz. can tomato sauce
4-oz. can green chiles
14 1/2-oz. can stewed tomatoes
1 can kidney beans
1 bay leaf

Sauté ground beef, onions, green pepper, jalapeño peppers and garlic in oil. Add chili powder, cumin, garlic salt and beer and let stand two minutes. Add hot sauce, tomato sauce, green chiles, stewed tomatoes, kidney beans and bay leaf. Cover and simmer on low heat for 3 hours. Remove bay leaf and serve with favorite cheese.

Sterling Rachwal
Winnebago, WI

SMOKED SAUSAGES & BEER

4 to 5 large red potatoes,
    cut into 1-inch cubes
3 to 4 medium yellow or red
    onions, cut into 1-inch chunks

16-oz. pkg. smoked sausage
1 bottle beer

Cover potatoes and onions with enough water to cover in a large skillet. Bring to a boil over medium heat until potatoes are tender. Add beer and prepared sausage. To prepare sausage, begin with beef sausage or any Polish or link sausage (not breakfast sausage). Cook on grill or broil in oven with or without barbecue sauce, or microwave on high for a minute and a half; sausage can be cooked ahead of time and refrigerated. Cut sausage into 1/2- to 3/4-inch pieces. Drain fat and add to potatoes, onion and beer. Serve with corn and more beer.

Kelly Kutz
North St. Petersburg, FL

STEAMED BAKE ON THE GRILL

12 jumbo shrimp
1¹/2 cup water
12 crab legs
5 dozen clams
4 ears corn
4 red potatoes
1 cup clam juice
1 cup chicken broth
1 cup shrimp stock
1 cup water
¹/2 cup white wine

¹/3 cup olive oil
4 T. butter
10 cloves garlic, chopped
1 large onion, quartered
Italian seasoning
Oregano
Bay seasoning
Lemon Pepper
Garlic powder
2 large aluminum foil roasting pans, one
   with handles, one without

Shell and devein shrimp, leaving tails on for looks. Place shells in 1 quart pan with 1¹/2 cup water; cover and cook on medium heat for about 15 minutes. Strain and reserve liquid to make 1 cup shrimp stock.

Rinse crab legs and scrub clams. Rinse corn and scrub potatoes; cut potatoes into quarters. Place heavy duty aluminum roaster without handles inside roaster with handles (doubled for strength). Spread clams, shrimp, crab legs, corn and potatoes evenly in roaster.

Combine clam juice, chicken broth, shrimp stock, 1 cup water, white wine, olive oil, butter, garlic and large onion. Add Italian seasoning, oregano, bay seasoning, lemon pepper and garlic powder to taste and pour mixture over ingredients in roaster. Cover with double sheet of wide aluminum foil and seal. Grill on high heat for 40 minutes with grill closed.

Robert Liiro
Easton, PA

PEPPERED RIB-EYE STEAKS

4 beef rib-eye steaks
1 T. olive or vegetable oil
1 T. garlic powder
1 T. paprika
2 tsp. dried thyme
2 tsp. dried oregano
1 tsp. salt
1 1/2 tsp. black pepper
1 tsp. lemon pepper
1 tsp. cayenne pepper

Prush steaks lightly with oil. Combine garlic powder, paprika, thyme, oregano, salt, black pepper, lemon pepper and cayenne pepper in small bowl. Sprinkle seasonings over steaks and press into both sides. Cover and refrigerate for 1 hour.

Grill steaks over medium heat, turning once. Grill 14 to 18 minutes for rare, 18 to 22 minutes for medium, 24 to 28 minutes for well done.

Edwin Siegel
Rush City, MN

CHILI CASSEROLE

1 lb. ground beef
2 T. vegetable oil
2 onions, sliced
1 clove garlic, crushed
15-oz. can red kidney beans
8 oz. can baked beans
1 tsp. chili powder
Salt and pepper
1 cup beef stock
1 T. cornstarch
2 T. water
Chopped parsley to garnish

Brown meat in oil and transfer to ovenproof casserole. Sauté onions and garlic in same skillet until lightly colored. Add onion, garlic and beans to casserole. Heat chili powder, salt, pepper and stock in skillet and bring to a boil. Pour over meat in casserole and cover tightly.

Bake at 325°F at 1 hour. Blend cornstarch with 2 tablespoons water and stir into casserole. Return to oven and bake an additional 20 to 30 minutes. Garnish with parsley and serve while hot with baked potato and crusty bread.

J.C. Scott
Summerville, SC

MOTHER'S DEPRESSION-ERA CHILI-MAC

3 lbs. lean ground beef
1 medium onion, chopped
1 bell pepper, chopped
2 tsp. allspice
2 tsp. nutmeg
2 tsp. salt
2 tsp. cinnamon
2 tsp. chili powder
1 tsp. minced garlic
4 (8-oz.) cans tomato sauce
4 cups water
1 lb. elbow macaroni

Brown meat, drain and set aside. Sauté onion and pepper in large cast iron skillet. Add spices, tomato sauce, water and macaroni and simmer for 5 minutes. Add meat and simmer 5 minutes more or until thoroughly warm.

Guy Claypool
Chapparal, NM

STROMBOLI

1 loaf frozen bread dough
2 egg yolks
1 T. Parmesan cheese
1 tsp. parsley
1/2 tsp. garlic powder
1 tsp. oregano
1/2 tsp. pepper
2 T. cooking oil
1/2 lb. pepperoni, sliced
12 oz. provolone or mozzarella cheese
2 egg whites, lightly beaten

Thaw bread dough and spread on greased cookie sheet to make crust. Mix egg yolks, Parmesan cheese, parsley, garlic powder, oregano, pepper and oil. Spread mixture on dough like butter. Cover with pepperoni and cheese.

Roll like a jelly roll, beginning at the narrow end and rolling the long way. Place seam side down and pinch ends closed. Brush with egg whites. Bake at 350°F for 30 to 40 minutes. Serve warm.

James Cornell
Bedford, PA

PIZZA PARLOR PIZZA

^{2}/$_3$ cup warm water
2 pkgs. yeast
2 tsp. sugar
2 cups cold water
3 T. cooking oil
1 tsp. salt

^{1}/$_4$ tsp. garlic salt
^{1}/$_2$ tsp. oregano
6^1/$_2$ to 7 cups all-purpose flour
^{1}/$_4$ cup oil
1 cup pizza sauce
Mozzarella cheese

Sprinkle yeast over warm water and stir in sugar; let stand for 5 minutes. Combine yeast mixture with cold water, oil, salt, garlic salt, oregano and 3 cups flour and stir. Work in remaining flour to form soft dough. Cover with light towel and let rise; when dough has doubled in size, divide into three portions. Pour ^{1}/$_4$ cup oil into 15-inch cast-iron skillet or large ovenproof frying pan. Roll dough on floured surface to size of skillet bottom. Spread 1 cup pizza sauce on crust. Cover with layer of cheese and toppings. Bake at 475°F to 490°F for 8 to 10 minutes. Sprinkle with more cheese during last 3 minutes of baking. Makes 3 pizzas.

• PIZZA PARLOR BREAD STICKS •

1 T. yeast
1^1/$_2$ cups warm water
1 T. oil
1^1/$_2$ tsp. salt
1 T. sugar
4 cups all-purpose flour

^{1}/$_2$ cup butter, melted
3 T. olive oil
3 T. Parmesan cheese
1 tsp. garlic powder
2 T. dried parsley

Dissolve yeast in warm water. Add oil, salt and sugar. Stir in flour until dough is too stiff to stir with a spoon. Turn onto floured surface and knead for several minutes. Cover with light towel and let rise until double in size. When dough is nearly risen, mix butter, olive oil, Parmesan cheese, garlic powder and parsley and set aside. When dough is doubled, roll into 15 x 15-inch square, using flour as needed for smooth rolling. Using pizza cutter, cut dough into strips and cut each strip into 5-inch lengths. Dip strips into butter mixture, twist and place on cookie sheets. Let rise and bake until golden brown. Delicious with pizza, warm pizza sauce, cheese dip or soup.

James Cornell
Bedford, PA

PORK TIKKI

1 lb. lean pork, cut into cubes
¹/4 cup plain yogurt
1-inch piece of gingerroot, peeled and finely grated
1 garlic clove, crushed
¹/2 tsp. paprika
Salt

Black pepper
Red food coloring (optional)
8 button mushrooms, trimmed
¹/2 red pepper, cut into 8 pieces
Vegetable, canola or olive oil

Mix yogurt, gingerroot, garlic, paprika, salt, pepper and, if desired, red food coloring. Add pork to marinade and toss well. Cover and refrigerate overnight or at least 3 hours.

When ready to cook, thread pork onto 4 long skewers, alternating with mushrooms and peppers. Brush with oil and barbecue for 12 to 14 minutes, turning several times and brushing with marinade at least once during cooking. Serve with rice and cole slaw.

J.C. Scott
Summerville, SC

ANNIE'S HAYSTACKS

Pinto beans
Ground meat (optional)
Favorite seasonings
Tortilla chips
Ripe tomatoes, chopped
Large onions, chopped

Lettuce, shredded
Cheddar cheese, grated
Salsa
Ranch dressing (optional)
Sour cream (optional)

Cook pinto beans according to package instructions. Brown ground meat, drain and season according to taste. Arrange tortilla chips on plate and cover with pinto beans. Pile on ground meat, tomatoes, onions, lettuce, cheese and salsa according to taste. If desired, add ranch dressing and/or sour cream.

Annie Christensen
Boulder, MT

Pork Tikki

DISHWASHER ISLAND

I made an island for the dishwasher so it would have a built-in appearance. I added receptacles to the island, trimmed it all out in wood blocks and made a tile worksurface. I made separate cabinets for the kitchen sink and a drop-in stove—these are only 30 inches high, which is just right for my wife, who is less than 5 feet tall. She sure loves her kitchen!

Elic H. Burks Jr.
St. Joseph, MO

COUNTRY-STYLE STEAK—THE CITY VERSION

4 pieces cube steak
Oil
Salt and coarse-ground pepper

Flour for dredging
Dry red wine or Madeira
10¾-oz. can beef broth

Heat a large (nonstick) fry pan before adding oil. While heating oil to smoking point, sprinkle meat liberally on both sides with salt and pepper and dredge in flour, shaking to remove excess. Brown meat well on both sides. Pour in a splash of red wine or Madeira to deglaze fry pan, scraping brown bits from bottom.

When bubbling stops, add beef broth and bring to a boil. Reduce heat to low, cover pan and simmer gently for about 1 hour or until meat is very tender. Remove meat from pan and reduce liquid until sauce reaches desired consistency. Pour over meat and serve with brown rice or mashed potatoes and favorite vegetable.

• BROWN RICE •

1 cup brown rice
2 T. butter
10¾-oz. can beef broth

Enough water to bring
    broth to 2 cups
Splash of white wine (optional)

Place rice, butter, beef broth and water, and wine (if desired) in small, stove proof casserole dish. Stir over medium heat until butter is melted. Cover and bake at 350°F for about 1 hour or until all liquid is absorbed. Top with a bit of sauce from Country-Style Steak.

Gene Brown
Raleigh, NC

OVEN VENISON STEW

1^1/2 lbs. venison or beef steak or stew meat
16-oz. can sliced mushrooms
5 large potatoes, quartered
10^1/2-oz. can cream of mushroom soup
1 T. Worcestershire
Salt and pepper

Line large iron skillet with aluminum foil, leaving enough to wrap over top of ingredients. Layer foil with venison or beef, mushrooms, potatoes. Top with mushroom soup. Splash Worcestershire sauce over everything and season to taste with salt and pepper.

Wrap aluminum foil tightly around ingredients. Pour water around edges of aluminum foil; foil package will float like a boat. Bake at 375°F for 2^1/2 hours. Check water level after 1^1/2 hours and add water if needed.

Nick Morrow
Dallas, GA

EASY CHICKEN CASSEROLE

16-oz. pkg. egg noodles
2 to 3 cups canned chicken breast
^{1}/2 cup margarine, melted
^{1}/2 cup flour
2 cups chicken broth
1^1/2 cups milk
10^1/2-oz. can condensed creamy mushroom soup
8 oz. processed American cheese, cubed
Potato chips, crushed

Cook egg noodles according to package directions; drain. Arrange noodles in lightly greased 9 x 13-inch pan. Arrange chicken over noodles. Mix margarine and flour. Add broth, milk, soup and cheese and stir. Pour over chicken and top with crushed potato chips. Bake at 350°F for 45 minutes.

Gordon Starr
Tucson, AZ

MEAT AND POTATOES DINNER

4 medium Wisconsin potatoes, peeled and
thinly sliced (about 4 cups)
1 lb. ground beef
1 cup seasoned bread crumbs
2/3 cup chopped onion
10-oz. bottle steak sauce
4 oz. cheddar cheese, shredded (about 1 cup)

Layer potatoes in lightly greased 9 x 9 x 2-inch baking pan and set aside. Mix ground beef, bread crumbs and onion in large bowl. Add steak sauce, reserving 2 tablespoons for later use. Mix well and spread evenly over potatoes, pressing firmly. Brush with 2 tablespoons steak sauce. Bake at 350°F for 1 hour and 15 minutes or until potatoes are tender. Sprinkle with cheese during last 5 minutes of cooking. Let stand 10 minutes before serving.

Andrew Gaylord
Ladd, IL

CHEESY CHOP BLOCKS

3 to 4 thick-cut pork chops or loin chops
Oil
1/2 cup muffin mix
1 egg
1/2 cup milk
1/2 cup bread crumbs
15-oz. can cheddar cheese soup
1 cup water
1 small onion
4 to 5 oz. real or imitation bacon bits

Cut chops into squares (or blocks) and brown in oil. Combine muffin mix, egg and milk in a bowl. Dip chops in muffin mixture, roll in bread crumbs and place immediately in baking dish. Bake at 350°F for 1 hour or until meat is no longer pink in center.

Combine soup with equal amount of water. Add chopped onion and bacon. Pour over chops and broil 5 minutes. Serve with cheesy sauce, which is good over mashed potatoes or as garnish for baked potato.

Donald T. Wagner
Tornado, WV

Buttermilk
Pound Cake

DESSERTS

BUTTERMILK POUND CAKE

$^1/_2$ cup shortening
$^1/_2$ cup butter, softened
$2^1/_2$ cups sugar
4 large eggs

1 tsp. vanilla
$^1/_2$ tsp. almond extract
3 cups flour
1 cup buttermilk

Grease and flour 10-inch Bundt pan. Cream shortening, butter and sugar until light. Add eggs one at a time, beating after each. Add vanilla and almond extract. Add flour, alternating with buttermilk, and mix until smooth. Spoon thick batter into Bundt pan with spatula. Poke batter to release air pockets, being careful not to touch spatula to sides of pan. Smooth top of batter. Bake at 325°F for 1 hour and 15 minutes or until toothpick inserted in center comes out clean. Remove from oven and cool in pan on cooling rack for 10 minutes. Invert onto serving plate and cool completely. Serve with sauce (below) or mixed berries or both.

• SAUCE •

1 cup whipping cream
1 cup sugar

$^1/_2$ cup butter

Bring cream and sugar to a boil, stirring often to dissolve sugar. Add butter, return to a boil, then remove from heat. Allow to cool about 15 minutes and stir before serving. Sauce will thicken as it cools. Spoon onto slices of Buttermilk Pound Cake.

Larry Lessmann
Oklahoma City, OK

BUCKEYES

2 lbs. peanut butter
3 lbs. powdered sugar
2 cups butter or margarine
$^2/_3$ slab of paraffin wax
6 oz. semi-sweet chocolate chips
6 oz. milk chocolate chips

Blend peanut butter, powdered sugar and butter. Roll into balls about 1-inch in diameter and refrigerate for 1 to 1$^1/_2$ hours. Melt paraffin and chocolate over hot water in double boiler. Dip peanut balls into chocolate.

Todd Jackson
Campbell, MO

OLD-FASHIONED TEA CAKES
(SUGAR COOKIES)

1 cup shortening
1 cup butter or margarine, softened
1 cup granulated sugar
1 cup powdered sugar
2 eggs
1 tsp. soda
1$^1/_2$ tsp. vanilla
4 cups all-purpose flour

Cream shortening, butter and sugars and beat well. Add eggs 1 at a time, beating well after each. Add soda and vanilla. Slowly add flour. Dough will become very stiff; can mix by hand if desired. Roll into small balls (or large if larger coolies are preferred) and place on lightly greased cookie sheet about 2 inches apart. Moisten bottom of smooth drinking glass with water and dip in granulated sugar; press each ball flat and thin. Bake at 350°F for about 7 minutes or until edges are light brown.

Tony Aaron
Milner, GA

PEANUT BUTTER FUDGE

2 cups sugar
3/4 cup evaporated milk
1 tsp. vanilla
1 cup peanut butter
2 cups marshmallow creme

Mix sugar and milk in saucepan and bring to a boil. Cook 4^1/$_2$ to 5 minutes over medium heat, stirring constantly. Remove from heat and add vanilla, peanut butter and marshmallow creme, stirring until well blended. Pour into buttered pan and cool slightly before cutting into squares.

Chuck Davis
Albany, MO

ORANGE BUTTERMILK SALAD

20-oz. can unsweetened
crushed pineapple, undrained
3 T. sugar
6-oz. pkg. orange gelatin (or any fruit flavor)
2 cups buttermilk
8-oz. frozen whipped dessert topping
1 cup chopped walnuts or pecans

Combine pineapple and sugar in saucepan and bring to a boil, stirring occasionally. When mixture boils, immediately add gelatin and stir until dissolved. Remove from heat. When cooled slightly, stir in buttermilk. Chill mixture until partially set. Fold in whipped topping and nuts and pour into lightly oiled 8^1/$_2$ cup mold. Chill overnight.

Jan Morrison
Visalia, CA

MAUI SUNRISE PIE

¹/₂ cup plus 1 T. orange drink mix
2 cups cold water
2 cups boiling water
6-oz. pkg orange gelatin
2 cups whipped dessert topping
2 large egg whites
¹/₄ tsp. salt
¹/₄ cup sugar
2 large graham cracker pie crusts

Mix orange drink mix in cold water. Stir gelatin into boiling water and stir for 2 minutes. Add orange drink mix, stir and chill until mix starts to gel. Fold in whipped dessert topping.

In separate bowl, mix egg whites and salt and beat until whites begin to foam. Gradually beat in sugar. Beat mixture until stiff peaks form. Fold into gelatin mixture and whip until creamy and smooth. When color is consistent, pour into pie crusts and chill.

Jerry Dawes
Perry, OK

CHOCOLATE CHIP COOKIE BARS

2 frozen chocolate chip cookie rolls
2 (8-oz.) pkgs. cream cheese, softened
¹/₂ cup butter
¹/₂ cup sugar
2 eggs, lightly beaten
1 tsp. vanilla

Slice 1 cookie roll into rounds and line bottom of greased 9 x 9-inch baking dish. Mix cream cheese, butter, sugar, eggs and vanilla and pour over cookie base. Slice second cookie roll and place on top of cream cheese mixture. Bake at 375°F for about 1 hour and 10 minutes.

Amy Nielsen
Plymouth, MN

BANANA WALNUT CAKE

^{2}/3 cup mashed banana

^{1}/2 cup light margarine, softened

Egg substitute, equivalent to 3 eggs

^{1}/2 cup sugar substitute

^{3}/4 cup water

2 cups unbleached white flour

1^1/4 tsp. baking powder

1 tsp. baking soda

1 tsp. cinnamon

^{1}/2 cup chopped walnuts

^{1}/2 cup raisins

Blend mashed banana and margarine in mixing bowl until creamy. Add egg substitute, sugar substitute and water and beat well. Sift flour, baking powder, baking soda and cinnamon. Stir into batter until smooth. Add walnuts and raisins and stir.

Coat 9 x 13-inch pan with nonstick vegetable spray, then dust with flour. Spread batter in pan, bake at 350°F for 20 minutes or until toothpick inserted in center of pan comes out clean.

Sterling Rachwal
Winnebago, WI

ROLLOUT CABINET SHELVES
TWO VARIATIONS

The "before" photo shows a cabinet with the usual problems: pots and pans stacked and hard to get to. To make it worse, the top shelf is only half a shelf.

To make things easily accessible, I removed the center stile and attached it to a door, which opens up the cabinet. When the door is closed, it looks the same as before—the cutline looks like a normal joint in the frame.

For the hardware, I used Blum bottom-mount, self-closing slides. The cabinet member slides are mounted on Blum brackets and then attached to the floor of the cabinet.

The upper cabinet member slide is mounted to oak blocks that are attached to the stiles in the front and to Blum brackets in the rear, mounted on the existing half shelves. The slides must be set behind the stiles so that when the door closes, the stile attached to the door will not hit the rollout (this is the reason for the oak blocks attached to the stile on the upper rollout).

I used 1/2" 9-ply Baltic Birch plywood for the 2"-high rollouts and 1/4" plywood for the bottoms. These rollouts are simple to construct or can be ordered from a local cabinetmaker or one of the many component suppliers around the country.

Lee Pfoutz
Plano, TX

Our kitchen cabinets did not have any space suitable for canned-good storage, so I remodeled part of the lower base cabinet with roll-out shelves using drawer slides. I used a thin-blade saw to cut the stile between the doors loose at top and bottom, then I glued it to the back of the right-hand door.

I framed the sides in with 1 × 2 frame and installed $^1/2$" plywood. I mounted the side-mount drawer slides to the plywood sides and the other half of each slide to the $^3/4$" plywood shelves.

The shelves needed back panels to keep cans or other items from falling off. The ell-brackets can be longer and mount on back and under. Because the bottom shelf is close to the bottom of the cabinet, I mounted a $3^1/2$" wood cabinet pull on the top front of the shelf so it could be easily pulled open.

Shelves can be spaced up or down as needed. Since these shelves will hold up to 100 pounds, they could be used in the shop also. Use slides that are the full length of the shelf—front to back—for more support and mount them under the edge. In the shop these can save a lot of work getting to tools or materials stored under the workbench.

Leslie Paugh Sr.
Corapeake, NC

RUM BALLS

10-oz. pkg. vanilla wafer cookies
1 cup pecans, finely chopped
1 cup powdered sugar
2 T. unsweetened cocoa
2 T. corn syrup
$^1/_3$ cup dark rum

Finely crush vanilla wafers with rolling pin. Mix crumbs with pecans, sugar and cocoa. Mix corn syrup and rum and mix into dry ingredients. Shape into tablespoon size balls. Roll in powdered sugar and store in tightly sealed container so flavors blend.

Kevin J. Dirth
Muscatine, IA

NO-BAKE CHOCOLATE OATMEAL COOKIES

2$^1/_2$ cups sugar
$^1/_2$ cup cocoa
$^1/_2$ cup milk
2 T. smooth peanut butter
1 tsp. vanilla
3 cups quick oats
$^1/_2$ cup chopped nuts (optional)

Stir sugar and cocoa together in large, heavy saucepan. Gradually add milk and bring to a rolling boil over medium heat; boil for 2 minutes.
Remove from heat and stir in peanut butter and vanilla. Add oats and nuts and mix well. Drop onto waxpaper with tablespoon and let cool.

Tony Aaron
Milner, GA

LEMON BARS

18¼- oz. box lemon cake mix
1 egg
½ cup butter, melted
8 oz. cream cheese, softened
1 lb. box powdered sugar
2 eggs

Mix cake mix, 1 egg and butter. Press into 9 x 13-inch cake plan. Mix cream cheese, powdered sugar and 2 eggs. Pour onto cake mix and bake at 325°F for 30 minutes. Cut into squares while still warm.

Ezra Hays
Jefferson, MO

LOW-CAL DESSERT

8-oz. block fat-free cream cheese, softened
2 cups skim milk
2 (3-oz). boxes fat-free and sugar-free
butterscotch instant pudding
8-oz. tub whipped topping
8-inch chocolate pie crust

Blend cream cheese with milk in large mixing bowl, adding milk slowly to thoroughly blend with cheese. Increase mixer speed to whip mixture for 1 to 2 minutes until foamy. Reduce mixer speed and slowly add pudding mix. Increase speed until mixture thickens around blades. Reduce speed and work with spatula. Add whipped topping and work in with spatula until thoroughly blended. (Can substitute any flavor instant pudding and any no-bake pie crust.)

Pour mixture into pie shell. Cover pie plate tightly and refrigerate pie for about 3 hours.

Herbert Blaies Jr.
Glasgow, KY

CHOCOLATE-COVERED CHERRIES

3 T. margarine
$1/2$ cup evaporated whole milk
1 tsp. vanilla
$1/4$ tsp. salt
$4^{1/4}$ cups powdered sugar
2 cups semisweet chocolate chips
3 tsp. paraffin
20 oz. maraschino cherries

Melt margarine, milk, vanilla and salt; remove from heat. Gradually add powdered sugar. Turn dough onto board and knead with powdered sugar until smooth. Pinch off piece and wrap around single cherry. Repeat and chill wrapped cherries. Melt chocolate chips with paraffin over water in double boiler to make dipping chocolate. Dip each cherry in dipping chocolate.

Kevin J. Dirth
Muscatine, IA

BUTTERMILK PIE

$1/4$ cup all-purpose flour
$1/2$ cup melted margarine
$1/2$ cup buttermilk
$1^{1/2}$ cups sugar
$1/2$ tsp. vanilla
3 eggs
1 unbaked pie shell

Mix flour, margarine, buttermilk, sugar, vanilla and eggs. Pour mixture into pie shell. Bake at 350°F for at least 30 minutes or until golden brown.

Curtis Norris
Magnolia, MS

Buttermilk Pie

LOUISE'S PRIZE-WINNING DANG GOOD PIE

6 T. butter or margarine, melted
3 eggs
3 T. flour
1¹/₂ cups sugar
1 cup crushed pineapple, drained
1 cup coconut flakes
Unbaked 10-inch pie shell

Mix margarine, eggs, flour, sugar, pineapple and coconut. Pour into unbaked pie shell. Bake 1 hour at 350°F until set and brown. Double recipe fills 3 (9-inch) shells.

M.A. Hardin
Brownsville, KY

BANANA SALAD

4 lbs. bananas, peeled
4 cups milk
21-oz. bottle salad dressing
8 oz. sweetened coconut
Leaf lettuce

Cut bananas in half crosswise. Mix milk and salad dressing, blending well. Dip each banana half into dressing mixture. Roll bananas in coconut. Place coated banana half on lettuce leaf.

Alton E. Mickle
Birmingham, AL

LOW-CAL CAKE

1-lb. box 1-step angel food cake mix
20-oz. can crushed pineapple, undrained
Low-fat whipped dessert topping

Pour cake mix into mixing bowl and stir in crushed pineapple, including juice. Pour into greased 9 x 12-inch pan and bake at 350°F for 25 to 30 minutes. Serve with whipped topping.

Earl C. Whittenmore Jr.
Saucier, MS

CHOCOLATE SHORTCAKE

2 cups all-purpose flour
2 cups sugar
1 cup butter or margarine
$^{1}/_{4}$ cup cocoa

1 cup water
$^{1}/_{2}$ cup buttermilk
2 eggs, beaten
1 tsp. vanilla

Mix flour and sugar in large mixing bowl. Melt butter in saucepan and stir in cocoa. Add water and bring to rolling boil over medium heat. Pour over flour mixture and beat well. Add buttermilk, eggs and vanilla and beat well. Pour into well-greased and floured 13 x 9 x 2-inch pan. Bake at 400°F for 25 minutes. Serve with Chocolate Shortcake Icing (below).

• ICING •

$^{1}/_{2}$ cup margarine
3 T. cocoa
6 to 10 T. milk

1-lb. box powdered sugar
1 tsp. vanilla
1 cup chopped nuts

Bring margarine, cocoa and milk to a boil. Remove from heat and add powdered sugar and vanilla. Stir well and add nuts. Pour over hot cake while icing is still hot.

Tony Aaron
Milner, GA

Peach Cobbler
with Blueberries

PEACH COBBLER WITH BLUEBERRIES

6 cups (about 3 lbs.) fresh peaches,
   peeled, pitted and sliced
2 cups fresh blueberries, rinsed
   and drained
$^1/_2$ cup granulated sugar
$^1/_2$ cup light brown sugar

$^1/_2$ cup all-purpose flour
$^1/_8$ tsp. cinnamon
$^1/_4$ tsp. salt
Pinch of ground nutmeg
Pinch of ground clove

· TOPPING ·

$1^1/_2$ cups rolled oats
$^1/_2$ cup light brown sugar
$^1/_4$ all-purpose flour

$^1/_8$ tsp. salt
$^1/_2$ cup butter, cut into small pieces

In large bowl, toss peaches and blueberries with granulated and brown sugar, flour and spices. Transfer to baking dish. In medium bowl, combine rolled oats, brown sugar, flour and salt. Cut in butter with a pastry blender or fork until mixture resembles coarse crumbs; do not over mix. Sprinkle topping evenly over fruit and bake at 350°F for 1 hour or until bubbly.

Kelly Kutz
North St. Petersburg, FL

HAWAII DELIGHT

1 French vanilla cake mix
20-oz. can crushed pineapple, liquid reserved
1 pkg. instant coconut cream pudding
3 bananas, sliced
8-oz. tub whipped dessert topping
$^1/_2$ bag flaked coconut
$^1/_2$ cup chopped nuts
10-oz. jar maraschino cherries

Make cake according to package directions, using reserved pineapple juice in place of water. Add water as necessary to make sufficient liquid. Do not overbake; bake only until cake springs back to a gentle touch.

When cake is cool, poke holes with wooden spoon handle. Prepare pudding according to package directions. Pour pudding over cake. Slice bananas onto pudding, then place pineapple over bananas. Gently spread whipped topping over cake and smother with coconut and nuts. Garnish with cherries.

Lesa and Mark Kilpatrick
Warren, AR

CRAZY CAKE

10-oz. pkg. large marshmallows
1 pkg. chocolate cake mix
5-oz. pkg. cherry-flavored gelatin
1 can cherry pie filling

Place marshmallows in bottom of greased 9 x 13-inch pan. Prepare chocolate cake mix according to package directions and pour over marshmallows. Mix gelatin with pie filling and spoon over batter. Bake at 350°F for 50 minutes.

Larry Shriver
Davenport, IA

FAST CARAMEL CORN

16 cups popped popcorn
1 cup dry roasted peanuts (optional)
4 T. margarine
$^1/_2$ cup brown sugar
$^1/_8$ cup corn syrup
$^1/_4$ tsp. baking soda
$^1/_2$ tsp. vanilla

Place popcorn and peanuts in large brown paper sack. Mix margarine, brown sugar and corn syrup in 4 cup glass measuring cup or microwave-safe bowl. Microwave on high for 4 minutes. Stir in baking soda and vanilla. Pour caramel mixture over popcorn and peanuts in bag. Close bag and shake. Microwave bag on high for $1^1/_2$ minutes. Shake bag and microwave again for $1^1/_2$ minutes. Shake one more time and serve.

Jeff Clapper
White, SD

HARRIETTE'S RUM CAKE

$18^1/_4$-oz. pkg. yellow cake mix
3-oz. pkg. French vanilla pudding mix
$^1/_2$ cup amber Eclipse Barbados Rum
$^1/_2$ cup vegetable oil
$^1/_2$ cup water
4 eggs
$^1/_2$ cup unsalted butter
1 cup sugar
4 T. dark rum
$^1/_4$ cup water

Mix cake mix, pudding mix, amber rum, oil and water. Add eggs one at a time, beating after each addition. Pour batter into greased tube cake pan and bake at 350°F for about 1 hour. Ten minutes before cake is done, melt unsalted butter (no substitutes) and add sugar, dark rum and water. Bring to a boil, stirring, and remove from heat.

Remove cake from oven and place on cooling rack. When cake has cooled slightly, lay newspaper below rack to catch drips. Pour hot sauce carefully over cake and let it soak in while cake cools. When cake has cooled, turn onto cake plate. Serve with coffee.

Can be made as 4 smaller cakes (reduce baking time to 50 minutes), wrapped in plastic and foil and given as gifts.

Gene Brown
Raleigh, NC

123

OATMEAL CARMELITAS

2 cups flour
1 tsp. baking soda
$^1/_2$ tsp. salt
$1^1/_2$ cups brown sugar
1 cup melted butter
2 cups rolled oats
1 cup chocolate chips
1 cup butterscotch chips
1 cup nuts
50 light-colored caramels
$^1/_2$ cup evaporated milk

Sift flour, baking soda and salt. Mix brown sugar, butter and rolled oats and stir into flour mixture. Pat $^1/_2$ of crumb mixture into 9 x 13-inch pan to form crust and bake at 350° for 7 to 10 minutes.

Mix chips and nuts and sprinkle over crust. Heat caramels and evaporated milk on low until caramels are melted. Pour over chips and nuts. Sprinkle with remaining half of crumb mixture and pat firmly. Bake for another 15 to 20 minutes. Cool and then chill 2 hours before cutting into squares.

JoeAn and Billy Clark
Walla Walla, WA

HARDINS' FRUIT CAKE

4 cups graham cracker crumbs
2 cups white sugar
4 eggs, beaten
1 cup margarine, melted
1 tsp. baking powder
1 cup milk
1 cup sweetened coconut flakes
1 cup chopped nuts (pecans, walnuts or hickory nuts)
2 pounds fruit cake fruit mix
Vanilla, rum or brandy to taste

Combine graham cracker crumbs, sugar, eggs, margarine, baking powder, milk, coconut flakes, nuts, cake mix and vanilla, rum or brandy. Pour mixture into 1 well-greased tube pan or 2 well-greased 3 x 5 x 9-inch loaf pans. Bake at 350°F for 45 minutes to 1 hour.

M.A. and Louise Hardin
Brownsville, KY

RHUBARB CRUNCH

$^3/_4$ cup all-purpose flour
$^3/_4$ cup rolled oats
$^1/_2$ cup brown sugar
6 T. melted butter
2 tsp. ground anise seed
1 tsp. cinnamon

3 cups chopped rhubarb
$^1/_2$ cup sugar
1 T. cornstarch
$^1/_2$ cup water
$^1/_2$ tsp. vanilla

In a small bowl, mix flour, oats, brown sugar, butter, anise and cinnamon. Press half of mixture into greased, 8-inch square pan. Spread rhubarb over crumb mixture. In small saucepan, stir sugar and cornstarch, adding water slowly and whisking to avoid lumps. Cook over medium heat 3 to 5 minutes or until clear and slightly thickened.

Remove from heat and stir in vanilla. Pour sauce over rhubarb and top with remaining half of crumb mixture. Bake at 350°F for 55 minutes or until rhubarb appears bubbly and topping is crunchy. Serve warm, or cool to room temperature.

Kelly Kutz
North St. Petersburg, FL

TIRAMISU

24 Italian ladyfingers
3 T. dark rum
1¹/₂ cups strong espresso
6 eggs, separated

3 T. sugar
1 lb. mascarpone cheese
2 oz. semisweet chocolate, grated

Combine 1 tablespoon dark rum with 1¹/₄ cups espresso. Dip each of 12 ladyfingers quickly into this mixture and arrange in a row on serving platter. Beat egg yolks with sugar until pale and frothy. Add mascarpone cheese, remaining 2 tablespoons rum and ¹/₄ cup espresso. Using clean beaters, beat egg whites until stiff but not dry. Fold into cheese mixture.

Spread half of mixture over ladyfingers and sprinkle with half of grated chocolate. Dip remaining ladyfingers quickly into remaining espresso mixture as before and arrange over first layer. Cover with remaining cheese mixture and sprinkle with remaining grated cheese. Cover with foil tent, being careful not to touch dessert, and refrigerate 6 hours before serving.

Variation: Omit rum and substitute 2 tablespoons each Marsala, Triple Sec and brandy and 1 teaspoon orange extract. Also see recipe for Eggless Tiramisu on page 129.

Gene Brown
Raleigh, NC

Tiramisu

FRUIT COCKTAIL CAKE

2 cups flour
2 tsp. baking soda
1 tsp. salt
2 cups sugar
2 eggs, beaten
16- or 17-oz.can fruit cocktail

• ICING •

1 cup evaporated milk
$^1/_2$ cup coconut
$^1/_2$ cup margarine
$^1/_2$ cup white sugar
$^1/_2$ cup nuts

Sift flour, baking soda, salt and sugar. Add eggs and fruit cocktail. Bake at 350°F until done.

For icing, mix evaporated milk, coconut, margarine and sugar in saucepan and cook until thickened. Add nuts. Cool slightly, then spread over cooled cake.

Larry Shriver
Davenport, IA

CHOCOLATE- PEANUT BUTTER "FOO-FOO" PIE

$^1/_2$ cup margarine
1 cup flour
$^2/_3$ cup dry roasted peanuts
$^1/_3$ cup peanut butter
8-oz. package cream cheese
1 cup powdered sugar
2 cups whipped topping
1 pkg. instant chocolate pudding
1 pkg. instant vanilla pudding
$2^3/_4$ cups cold milk
$^2/_3$ cup dry roasted peanuts, chopped

Process margarine, flour and $^2/_3$ cup peanuts in food processor until ingredients are thoroughly mixed and coarse dough is formed. Press into greased 10-inch pie plate. Bake at 350°F for 20 minutes; cool.

Cream peanut butter, cream cheese and powdered sugar. Add 1 cup whipped topping and spread in cooled crust. Beat together puddings and milk and spread over first layer. Spread 1 cup whipped topping over second layer and sprinkle with chopped peanuts. Refrigerate until ready to serve.

Lesa and Mark Kilpatrick
Warren, AR

EGGLESS TIRAMISU

24 Italian ladyfingers
8 T. dark rum
1^1/$_2$ cups strong espresso
1 lb. mascarpone cheese
3 cups heavy cream or whipping cream
1^1/$_2$ cups plus 2 T. powdered sugar
1 tsp. vanilla extract
1 T. unsweetened cocoa
^{1}/$_2$ oz. semisweet chocolate, grated

Combine 4 tablespoons dark rum with 1^1/$_4$ cups espresso. Dip each of 12 ladyfingers quickly into this mixture and arrange in a row on serving platter. Process mascarpone cheese with several pulses in food processor until smooth. Add cream, 1^1/$_2$ cups sugar, remaining 4 tablespoons rum and ^{1}/$_4$ cup espresso. Spread half this mixture over dipped ladyfingers. Grate ^{1}/$_2$ of chocolate over this. Mix remaining 2 tablespoons sugar with cocoa and sprinkle generously over ladyfingers. If desired, add espresso powder to the mix. Repeat with second layer of ladyfingers, cheese mixture, and so on. Cover with foil tent, being careful not to touch dessert, and refrigerate 6 hours before serving.

Gene Brown
Raleigh, NC

WHOOPIE PIE CAKE

1 cup shortening
2 cups sugar
2 eggs
2^1/2 cups flour
^{1}/2 cup cocoa
2 tsp. baking soda

^{1}/2 tsp. salt
1 cup milk
1 T. vinegar
1 cup boiling water
1 tsp. vanilla

Cream shortening, sugar and eggs. Sift flour, cocoa, baking soda and salt and stir into batter. Add milk and vinegar and mix. Add boiling water and vanilla. Pour into 2 well-greased 10-inch round baking pans. Bake at 350°F for 15 to 20 minutes or until toothpick inserted in center comes out clean. Cool and frost with Whoopie Pie Frosting (below).

• WHOOPIE PIE FROSTING •

1^1/2 cups milk
^{1}/2 cup plus 1 T. flour
3 cups shortening

2^1/2 cups sugar
1 T. vanilla

Mix milk and flour in small saucepan. Cook over medium heat until paste is formed. Refrigerate until cool. In mixing bowl, combine paste, shortening, sugar and vanilla; mix on high until fluffy. Frost cake.

Ralph Guay Jr.
Old Town, ME

BUTTER CREAM FROSTING

¹/₂ cup milk
3 T. flour
¹/₂ cup shortening
¹/₂ cup sugar
1 tsp. vanilla
Fruit for flavoring (optional)

Combine milk and flour and cook over low heat until thickened. Beat shortening, sugar and vanilla together until creamy. Add flour and milk mixture and continue beating until fluffy. Add color or flavoring if desired. Frosts 8-inch layer cake or pan cake.

Kenneth Jabczynski Sr.
Burnham, IL

SNICKERDOODLES

1 cup margarine
1¹/₂ cups sugar
2 eggs
2³/₄ cups flour
1 tsp. soda
2 tsp. cream of tartar
¹/₂ tsp. salt
1 T. cinnamon
3 T. granulated sugar

Cream margarine and sugar; add eggs and beat. Sift flour, soda, cream of tartar and salt and stir into batter. Mix cinnamon with 3 tablespoons sugar. Roll dough into balls, roll balls in cinnamon and sugar. Bake at 350°F for 10 minutes.

Todd Jackson
Campbell, MO

BREAD PUDDING FOR A CROWD
(SERVES 50)

2 lbs. day-old bread, cut in $^1/_2$-inch cubes
2 sticks butter or margarine, melted
15 eggs, slightly beaten
3 cups sugar
1 T. salt
$^1/_4$ T. ground nutmeg
2 T. vanilla
$1^1/_2$ gallons milk
$1^1/_2$ lb. raisins
$^1/_4$ lb. chopped mixed nuts (pecans and walnuts)

Preheat oven to 350°F. Evenly distribute bread cubes into 2 greased pans. Pour margarine or butter over bread cubes, dividing butter evenly between the 2 pans. Toss the bread cubes lightly; toast in oven until light brown.

In an oversized bowl, mix eggs, sugar, salt, nutmeg and vanilla thoroughly; add milk to egg mixture and stir. Pour about 4 quarts of liquid over bread cubes in each pan. Add about 3 cups of raisins to each pan; top with chopped nuts. Bake for 15 minutes, then stir to distribute raisins and nuts. Continue baking for another 45 minutes or until firm.

Variation: For chocolate chip bread pudding, omit raisins, substituting 18 ounces of semi-sweet chocolate chips for each pan. Bake for 1 hour or until firm; do not stir during baking.

Alton E. Mickle
Birmingham, AL

BETTY'S BLUEBERRY BUCKLE

2 cups flour
$^1/_2$ cup sugar
1 T. baking powder
1 tsp. salt
1 egg
$^1/_2$ cup oil
1 cup milk
16-oz. can blueberries
$^1/_2$ cup sugar
$^1/_2$ cup flour
1 tsp. cinnamon
$^1/_4$ cup margarine, softened

Sift flour, sugar, baking powder and salt. Mix egg, oil and milk and blend into dry ingredients. Gently fold in blueberries with juice. Mix sugar, flour, cinnamon and margarine until crumbly to make topping. Pour batter into greased 9 x 13-inch cake pan and sprinkle with topping. Bake at 350°F for about 40 minutes.

Tim Graham
Moab, UT

VANILLA FLUFF

1 pkg. yellow cake mix
2 (3-oz.) pkgs. instant vanilla pudding mix
4 cups milk
8-oz. pkg. cream cheese, warmed
to room temperature
16-oz. can cherry pie filling
12-oz. tub frozen whipped topping
Colored coconut or chopped nuts

Bake cake according to package directions in 9 x 13-inch pan. Cool.

Combine both packages pudding and add 3$^1/_2$ cups milk. Mix softened cream cheese with $^1/_2$ cup milk. Combine pudding and cream cheese mixtures. Spread over cooled cake.

Top with evenly arranged cherries and spread with whipped topping. Sprinkle with coconut or nuts. Chill overnight.

Hilda Hoffmann
Preston, MN

BLUEBERRY-ORANGE CHEESECAKE

3¹/₂ cups graham cracker crumbs
5 T. granulated sugar
1¹/₄ tsp. cinnamon
1¹/₄ tsp. nutmeg
⁷/₈ cup butter
7 cups creamy cottage cheese
12 eggs
3 cups granulated sugar
8-oz. pkg. cream cheese, softened

1¹/₂ cups heavy cream
¹/₂ cup all-purpose flour
¹/₄ tsp. salt
2 T. vanilla
8 T. orange juice concentrate
2 cups sour cream
5 T. powdered sugar
2¹/₃ cups frozen blueberries, thawed

Combine graham cracker crumbs, sugar, cinnamon and nutmeg in bowl. Stir in butter with wooden spoon. Press mixture into bottom of 9-inch springform cake pan and ³/₄ of the way up the sides. Drain cottage cheese and set aside. Beat eggs in large mixing bowl until very thick. Add sugar, beating until light and fluffy. Blend in cottage cheese, cream cheese, cream, flour, salt, vanilla and orange juice concentrate. Mix well and turn into graham cracker crust.

Bake at 350°F for 1 hour and 10 to 20 minutes. Cheesecake is done when a table knife inserted in center comes out clean. While cake is baking, combine sour cream, powdered sugar and blueberries in small bowl. Turn off heat and remove cake when done. Gently spread cake with topping and return to turned-off oven. Cool in oven until cake is room temperature. Chill before serving.

James Mullen
East Meredith, NY

135

FIVE-LAYER DESSERT
NEXT BEST THING TO A HANDYMAN

1 cup all-purpose flour
1 cup chopped nuts
1/2 cup butter, melted
8 oz. cream cheese
1 cup sugar

12-oz. whipped dessert topping
3 cups milk
5-oz. box chocolate instant pudding
5-oz. box vanilla instant pudding
1 Hershey's chocolate bar

LAYER 1: Mix flour, nuts and butter and pat into greased 9 x 13-inch pan. Bake at 350°F for 10 minutes or until golden. Cool.

LAYER 2: Beat together cream cheese, sugar and half of whipped dessert topping. Spread on first layer.

LAYER 3: Beat together 1 1/2 cups milk and chocolate instant pudding and pour over second layer.

LAYER 4: Beat together 1 1/2 cups milk and vanilla instant pudding and pour over third layer.

LAYER 5: Spread remaining half of whipped dessert topping on fourth layer. Grate Hershey's bar onto whipped topping. Refrigerate for 2 hours before serving.

Randy Goodwin
Columbia, TN

MAYONNAISE CAKE

2 cups flour
2 tsp. baking soda
1^1/2 cups sugar
4 tsp. cocoa
^{1}/2 tsp. salt
1 tsp. vanilla
1 cup hot water
1 cup mayonnaise or whipped salad dressing
^{1}/3 cup nuts (optional)

Sift flour, soda, sugar, cocoa and salt together. Add vanilla, water and mayonnaise. Add nuts if desired. Bake at 350°F for 25 minutes in greased and floured 11 x 14-inch cake pan.

George A. Edelberg
Great Falls, MT

EGG YOLK COOKIES

12 egg yolks
1 cup brown sugar
1 cup white sugar
1^1/3 cups butter or margarine
2 tsp. vanilla
3^1/2 cups flour
1 tsp. baking soda
2 tsp. baking powder
1 tsp. salt
1 cup rolled oats
^{3}/4 cup coconut
^{1}/2 cup chopped nuts
^{3}/4 cup chocolate chips

Beat egg yolks until lemon colored. Cream sugar and butter until fluffy. Add beaten egg yolks and vanilla. Sift flour, baking soda, baking powder and salt and add to creamed batter. Add rolled oats, coconut, nuts and chocolate chips. Drop by teaspoon on lightly greased cookie sheet. Bake at 350°F for 12 minutes.

Donna Wenthold
Cresco, IA

KITCHEN REMODELING

When we decided to build this kitchen, we looked at everything we could find that had anything to do with kitchens. We found a little here and there that we liked, so we borrowed a lot of different ideas. But when it came to obtaining the correct hardware and cabinetry to do what we wanted, it was not to be found. So our custom design meant custom-made cabinets. Fortunately for us, Phil was able to make our designs a reality himself. For example, the base cabinets in this "L" are 40 inches high to accommodate our own height; the corner Lazy Susan is a full 34 inches in diameter, allowing us to use the entire corner with as little wasted space as possible; the lower cabinets are all drawers (except for the Lazy Susan cabinet) and are on 24-inch, full-extension drawer guides. All cabinets are constructed using plate joinery (biscuits). All cabinets and drawers are ³/₄" AA oak plywood with edge tape (we didn't use any particleboard).

Phil & Nita Taylor
Heber Springs, AR

We both do a lot of cooking. One of our pet peeves was trying to find a particular spice when we wanted it without digging through deep cabinets or losing them off of carousels. Coffee cups were always getting chipped from trying to stack them on top of each other to utilize the deep space between shelves in the normal cabinets. These "drawers" fill in the small space on either side of the upper corner Lazy Susan.

Each Lazy Susan carousel is topped with plastic laminate to match the countertop. Because of the size of the lower cabinet (36"), Phil customized the roller guides so they would glide easily and bear the weight of the heavy appliances we wanted to store. There are also lights on each "shelf" of the lower cabinet to make it easier to find things. The upper shelf in the upper Lazy Susan cabinet can be adjusted upward or downward.

The under-the-sink "drawers" are big enough to house the 13-gallon trash can on one side and have all those normally hard-to-find kitchen cleaners at our fingertips in the other drawer.

Deep, divided drawers are fully adjustable to accommodate different sizes of bowls and serving dishes. Fine, glass serving dishes are no longer in danger of being chipped from being stacked on top of each other to "save shelf space."

Wide, deep, fully-extended drawers make finding the right pot and lid a snap, without standing on your head or crawling into a dark cabinet.

Two of the vertical pantry drawers— fully loaded and they glide in and out with fingertip ease.

The "rear" pantry drawer.

COCONUT-LEMON COOKIES

1 cup vegetable shortening
1 1/2 cups sugar
2 large eggs
1 cup flaked coconut
3 T. lemon juice
3 cups all-purpose flour
2 tsp. cream of tartar
1 tsp. baking soda

Cream shortening and sugar in mixing bowl; beat in eggs. Add coconut and lemon juice; mix. Sift flour, cream of tartar and baking soda and blend into mixture.

Drop by teaspoonful 2 inches apart on ungreased cookie sheet. Bake at 400°F for 10 minutes or until edges are lightly browned. Remove from cookie sheet immediately.

Gary Mallon
Post Falls, ID

MOTHER'S LOVE APPLE PUDDING

4 to 6 baking apples
1/2 cup sugar
1/4 cup water
Sprinkle of cinnamon
1/4 cup butter, softened
1/2 cup sugar
1 egg
1 cup flour
1 tsp. baking powder
2/3 cup milk

Peel and slice apples and arrange in 9-inch buttered baking pan. Sprinkle with 1/2 cup sugar, water and cinnamon. Blend butter, sugar and egg in mixing bowl. Sift flour and baking powder and stir into batter. Add milk, stir, and pour over apples. Do not stir. Bake at 350°F for 45 minutes. Serve warm with cream.

Dot Strausser
Schuylkill Haven, PA

PLUM DUMPLINGS

4 medium potatoes
3 large eggs
Salt
3¼ cups all-purpose flour
20 German or Stanley plums, washed and pitted
¾ to 1 cup bread crumbs
¼ cup butter
Sugar

Cook potatoes with peels; cool, peel and grate or mash to make about 2 cups. (Can use instant potatoes if desired.) Add eggs and salt. Stir in flour, adding only enough to make a nice dough. Divide in half and roll out first half to about 15 inches wide, then roll up like salami. Cut roll into 10 pieces about 1½ inches thick. Flatten each piece with your hand. Put plum in center and wrap dough around to form ball; pinch closed. Repeat with other half. Add flour if necessary if dough becomes sticky.

Drop dough into large pan of boiling water. Cook for about 15 minutes or until dumplings rise to the top; drain. While dumplings are cooking, fry bread crumbs in butter. Sprinkle over dumplings when done, with sugar to taste.

John J. Tengelitsch
Buchanan, MI

RHUBARB FOAM

2 cups rhubarb, washed and
   cut into pieces
3/4 cup water
3/4 cup sugar

1 T. cornstarch
3 large egg whites
1/4 tsp. vanilla
3 medium bananas

Boil rhubarb in water until tender. Mix sugar and cornstarch and stir into boiled rhubarb until mixture starts to thicken. Beat egg whites. Add vanilla to egg whites and fold rhubarb into egg whites. Serve very cold with bananas.

Kevin J. Dirth
Muscatine, IA

IRISH CREAM

1 quart half and half
2 eggs
3 T. chocolate syrup
1¹/₂ cups whiskey
5 T. water
1 can sweetened condensed milk

Mix half and half, eggs, chocolate syrup, whiskey and water in large bowl and whip. Add milk last; whip. Serve in liqueur glasses.

Ken Goerdt
Hibbing, MN

APPLESAUCE CAKE IN A JAR

²/₃ cup shortening
2²/₃ cup sugar
4 eggs
3 cups applesauce
3¹/₃ cup flour
¹/₂ tsp. baking soda
1 tsp. cinnamon
1 tsp. ground clove

Cream shortening, sugar and eggs. Beat in applesauce. Sift dry ingredients and add to applesauce mixture, stirring just until mixed. Heavily grease 8 wide-mouth, oven safe pint canning jars. Fill jars half full. Bake at 325°F for 45 minutes.

Remove jars one at a time from oven. Wipe sealing rim clean and cover with lid and ring. Screw tight. Jars will seal as cake cools. Store as you would any canned goods.

James Cornell
Bedford, PA

OATMEAL RAISIN COOKIES

1 cup shortening
1 cup sugar
2 eggs
1/4 cup milk
2 cups flour
1/4 tsp. soda
1 heaping tsp. baking powder
1/2 tsp. nutmeg
1/2 tsp. cinnamon
1/4 tsp. cloves
2 cups rolled oats
1 cup raisins
1 cup chopped nuts

Beat shortening, sugar and eggs. Add milk. Sift flour with soda, baking powder, nutmeg, cinnamon and cloves and stir into batter. Add rolled oats, raisins, nuts and mix thoroughly. Drop by teaspoonful onto greased cookie sheet. Bake at 375°F for 5 to 10 minutes.

Hilda Hoffmann
Preston, MN

SPUMA DI CIOCCOLATA
CHOCOLATE MOUSSE

8 oz. semisweet chocolate,
cut into small pieces
3 eggs
3 to 4 T. dark rum
1 cup whipping cream
Additional cream, whipped
Grated chocolate

Melt chocolate by placing in small ovenproof bowl in oven at 200°F for 4 to 5 minutes. Remove chocolate and set aside. Beat eggs in medium bowl until foamy. Add dark rum. Beat 1 cup of cream in large bowl until stiff. Beat eggs and add gradually to cooled chocolate, beating at low speed to avoid over-beating. Fold chocolate mixture thoroughly into whipped cream.

Spoon mousse into 6 individual dessert glasses (or single glass bowl if preferred). Garnish with additional whipped cream and grated chocolate. Refrigerate overnight and serve chilled.

Gene Brown
Raleigh, NC

REFRIED BEAN CAKE

2 cups biscuit mix
3 tsp. baking powder
$^1/_2$ tsp. salt
$1^1/_2$ cups sugar
1 tsp. cinnamon
$^1/_2$ cup shortening, melted

2 eggs, beaten
$^1/_2$ cup grated Granny Smith
  or other apple
$^1/_2$ cup raisins
$1^1/_2$ refried beans
$^3/_4$ cup milk

Blend biscuit mix, baking powder, salt, sugar and cinnamon. Blend shortening, eggs, apple, raisins, refried beans and milk. Add gradually to biscuit mixture, stirring by hand until all ingredients are well mixed. Pour into greased, lightly floured 9 x 13-inch pan. Bake at 350°F for 40 to 50 minutes or until toothpick inserted in center comes out clean. Ice with Cream Cheese Frosting (below).

• CREAM CHEESE FROSTING •

$^1/_2$ cup butter or margarine
8-oz. pkg cream cheese, softened

1 tsp. vanilla
1-lb. box powdered sugar

Beat butter and cream cheese until well blended. Add vanilla. Slowly add powdered sugar and mix until smooth and creamy.

Robert Galeana
Imperial Beach, CA

DR. PEPPER CAKE

18 ³/4-oz. box cherry supreme cake mix
3-oz. box butter pecan instant
   pudding mix

10 oz. Dr. Pepper
4 eggs
¹/2 cup vegetable oil

• ICING •

2 eggs
1¹/2 cups sugar
3 T. cornstarch
¹/2 cup margarine

1 tsp. almond extract
1 cup chopped almonds
1 cup flaked coconut

Mix ingredients together and bake in three round layer pans at 350°F according to cake mix instructions or until toothpick inserted in center comes out clean. Allow to cool before icing.

For icing, mix eggs, sugar, cornstarch and margarine in saucepan and cook over low heat until thickened. Add almond extract, almonds and coconut. Beat until proper consistency for spreading.

M.A. Hardin
Brownsville, KY

REMODELED KITCHEN LAYOUT

By reconfiguring her kitchen layout, Jan Omernik of Steven's Point, Wisconsin created additional seating and food preparation space with no loss of kitchen function—and, in the process, she even created enough space for a small pantry.

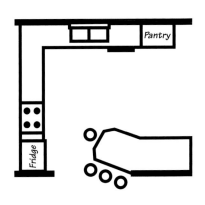

Removing part of her kitchen wall allowed Jan to build a bigger dining bar and create a more open kitchen area. Jan moved the original bar and built a pantry in its place.

Moving the fridge gave Jan the opportunity to make the changes she wanted in her kitchen.

Before

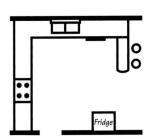

FOUR-LAYER CHOCOLATE CARAMEL CANDY

1 cup semisweet chocolate chips
1/2 cup butterscotch chips
3/4 cup creamy peanut butter
1/4 cup butter
1 cup sugar
1/4 cup evaporated whole milk
1 1/2 cup marshmallow creme

1 tsp. vanilla
1 1/2 cups salted peanuts, chopped
14-oz. pkg. caramels
1/4 cup whipping cream
1 cup milk or semisweet chocolate chips

Combine 1 cup chocolate chips, 1/4 cup butterscotch chips and 1/4 cup peanut butter in saucepan. Stir over low heat until melted. Spread on bottom of lightly greased 9 x 13-inch pan. Refrigerate until set. Meanwhile, melt butter and stir in sugar and evaporated whole milk (do not use fat-free). Bring to a boil and stir continuously while boiling for 5 minutes. Remove from heat.

Stir in marshmallow creme, 1/4 cup peanut butter and vanilla. Add peanuts. Spread over first layer and refrigerate until set. Combine caramels and whipping cream in saucepan over low heat, stirring constantly until melted and smooth. Spread over filling and refrigerate until set. Combine 1 cup milk or semisweet chocolate chips, 1/4 cup butterscotch chips and 1/4 cup peanut butter in saucepan. Stir over low heat until melted and smooth. Pour over caramel layer and refrigerate at least 1 hour. Cut into 1-inch squares. Store in refrigerator.

Amy Nielsen
Plymouth, MN

PUMPKIN PIE

2 cups pumpkin, prepared as below
1 cup half and half
$^1/_2$ cup sweetened condensed milk
$^1/_4$ brown sugar
$^1/_4$ cup white sugar
$^1/_2$ tsp. salt
2 eggs, slightly beaten
2 tsp. pumpkin pie spice
Unbaked 9-inch pie crust

Wash pumpkin and cut up, removing strings and seeds. Bake at 350°F for 1 hour or more until tender. Peel skin off and mash pumpkin flesh.

Mix 2 cups pumpkin with half and half, sweetened condensed milk, brown sugar, white sugar, salt, eggs and pumpkin pie spice. Pour into unbaked pie crust and bake at 350°F for 1 hour or until knife inserted in pie comes out clean.

Kelly Kutz
North St. Petersburg, FL

FRESH FRUIT SALAD

2 cups water
1 cup sugar
1 tsp. lemon juice
Fresh fruit, cut into pieces

Combine water, sugar and lemon juice. Bring to a boil and boil for 5 minutes. Cool completely. Add fresh fruit pieces to simple syrup mixture. Cover and store in refrigerator until ready to serve.

James Cornell
Bedford, PA

GRANDMA'S OREO DESSERT

1¹/₂-lb. bag Oreo cookies
¹/₄ to ¹/₂ cup butter
¹/₂ gallon cookies-and-cream ice cream
8-oz. jar hot fudge sauce
12-oz. container whipped dessert topping

Crush 2¹/₂ rows of Oreos in a food processor (or on a cookie sheet with a rolling pin) until finely grated. Remove ice cream from freezer to soften. Melt butter. Pour cookie crumbs into a 9 x 13-inch pan. Add enough melted butter to cookies until crumbs become firm enough to form the bottom of the dessert. Press cookies together evenly over the pan-bottom and freeze for about 15 minutes.

Remove pan from freezer and spread ice cream evenly over crumbs. Freeze again until ice cream is firm (about 15 minutes).

Heat fudge in microwave for a few minutes at a time until it is fairly smooth and easy to stir. Pour hot fudge over ice cream. (The fudge tends to clump, but just spread it as best you can, keeping it fairly even over the entire pan.) Freeze until fudge is firm.

Remove pan from freezer and spread whipped dessert topping evenly over fudge layer. Crush remaining ¹/₂ row of cookies; top the dessert with crushed Oreos. Remove dessert from freezer 10 to 15 minutes prior to serving.

Molly Hollenbeck
Eden Prairie, MN

PINEAPPLE CHEESE PIE

20-oz. can crushed pineapple
1 small box pineapple gelatin
16-oz. cream cheese
12-oz. whipped dessert topping
9-inch unbaked pie crust

Drain juice from pineapple, reserving juice. Dissolve gelatin in pineapple juice; microwave for 1 minute or heat to 180°F. Mix cream cheese with whipped topping and add pineapple. Pour gelatin mixture into cream cheese mixture and mix well. Pour into pie shell and refrigerate for 4 to 5 hours.

James R. Bray
Fresno, CA

SCRATCH CHOCOLATE PUDDING MIX

4 cups nonfat dry milk powder
$2^2/3$ cups sugar
$1^1/3$ cups cornstarch
1 cup unsweetened cocoa
$^1/2$ tsp. salt

Stir all ingredients until well-mixed. Store in tightly covered container at room temperature. Stir or shake mix before each use.

• CHOCOLATE PUDDING •

1 cup chocolate scratch pudding mix
2 cups water
1 T. butter or margarine
$^1/2$ tsp. vanilla

In medium saucepan, stir pudding mix and water until well blended. For richer, creamier pudding, substitute 2 cups milk for 2 cups water. For mocha pudding, substitute 1 cup strong black coffee for 1 cup water. Bring to a boil over medium heat, stirring constantly. Boil for 1 minute. Stir in butter or margarine and vanilla. Pour into individual bowls and chill.

Doris Swihart
Heron, MT

GRANDMA'S OLD-FASHIONED SHORTNIN' BREAD COOKIES

¹/₂ cup butter, softened
¹/₄ cup light brown sugar
1¹/₂ cups flour

Cream butter and sugar. Add flour and roll mixture out quickly on a floured board to ¹/₂-inch thickness. Cut dough with small biscuit cutter and place on lightly greased and floured cook sheet. Bake at 350°F for about 20 minutes or until golden brown. For a delicious variation, substitute ¹/₄ cup ground hazelnuts for ¹/₄ cup of flour.

Doris Swihart
Heron, MT

BLUEBERRY OR RASBERRY CREAM MUFFINS

4 cups flour
1 tsp. baking soda
2 tsp. baking powder
1 tsp. salt
4 eggs
2 cups sugar
1 cup vegetable oil
1 tsp. vanilla
2 cups sour cream
2 cups blueberries (or raspberries)

Sift flour, baking soda, baking powder and salt and set aside. Beat eggs and sugar together. Add oil and vanilla to eggs. Slowly fold in dry ingredients, alternating with sour cream. Gently fold in berries.

Bake at 400°F for 20 minutes or until toothpick inserted in center of muffin comes out clean.

Todd Jackson
Campbell, MO

OREO PEANUT FUDGE DESSERT

1½-lb. pkg. Oreo cookies
½ melted butter
½ gallon vanilla ice cream, softened
2½ cups Spanish peanuts
2 cups powdered sugar

12-oz. can evaporated milk
1 cup chocolate chips
½ cup butter
1 tsp. vanilla
8 oz. whipped dessert topping

Finely crush cookies and mix with melted butter. Press into 9 x 13-inch pan and refrigerate. Spread softened ice cream over cookie crumbs and sprinkle with peanuts. Pack well and smooth the surface. Cover and freeze.

Combine sugar, milk, chocolate chips and butter in saucepan and bring to a boil. Cook for 8 minutes, stirring constantly. Remove from heat and stir in vanilla. Allow to cool and pour over frozen ice cream in pan. Spread whipped dessert topping over chocolate. Cover and freeze.

Ken Goerdt
Hibbing, MN

APPLE CRUMB PIE

6 tart apples
1 cup sugar
³/₄ cup flour

¹/₃ cup butter
1 tsp. cinnamon
Unbaked 9" pie crust

Peel and core apples and cut into thick slices. Mix ¹/₂ cup sugar with cinnamon and 1 T. of flour; sprinkle over apples. Arrange in unbaked pie shell. Blend remaining flour with ¹/₂ cup sugar and butter and work into small crumbs with fork or fingers. Sprinkle crumbs over apples.

Bake at 425°F for 10 minutes; reduce heat to 350°F and continue baking for 35 minutes or until apples are tender and crust is golden.

• NO-FAIL PIE CRUST •

4 cups flour
1 T. sugar
Dash salt
1¹/₂ cups shortening

1 egg, beaten well
1 tsp. vinegar
¹/₂ cup water

Mix flour, sugar and salt. Work in shortening until mixture looks like coarse oatmeal. Add beaten egg, vinegar and water. Mix lightly and divide into four parts for 2 large two-crust pies or 4 one-crust pies, or into 6 parts for 3 small two-crust pies or 6 single crust pies. Fill with your favorite pie filling. Bake at 450°F for 10 minutes; reduce heat to 250°F and continue baking for 35 to 40 minutes.

James Cornell
Bedford, PA

SCRATCH PUDDING MIX

4 cups nonfat dry milk powder
1 1/3 cups sugar
1 cup cornstarch
1/2 tsp. salt

Stir all ingredients until well-mixed. Store in tightly covered container at room temperature. Stir or shake mix before each use.

• VANILLA PUDDING •

1 cup scratch pudding mix
2 cups water
2 T. butter or margarine
1 tsp. vanilla

In medium saucepan, stir pudding mix and water until well blended. Bring to a boil over medium heat, stirring constantly. Boil for 1 minute. Stir in butter or margarine and vanilla. Pour into individual bowls and chill.

Doris Swihart
Heron, MT

CHERRIES JUBILEE, C. 1709

1-lb. can sour cherries
1/2 cup honey or sugar
2 T. arrowroot
1 T. cornstarch
1/2 tsp. almond extract
Red food coloring (optional)

Pour juice from cherries into measuring cup. Add enough water to make 1 1/2 cups and pour into saucepan. Add honey or sugar and boil for 5 minutes. Mix arrowroot and cornstarch in small amount of water to make paste. Add paste to boiling mixture. Stir until thickened. Add almond extract and stir well. Add cherries. If desired, add a little red food coloring.
Serve in individual cups or pour over ice cream.

William Leistner
Maryville, TN

ADD-ON TABLE

T ired of seating your extra dinner guests at the wobbly card table that's several inches lower than your dining room table? I was, so I built this portable add-on table that accommodates four more guests. I made it of $1/2" \times 4' \times 4'$ A-B plywood cut down to meet my existing dining table. It's finished with one coat of stain and two coats of polyurethane.

After dinner, I can break down the table and stow it in the garage.

Joe Flynn
Port St. Lucie, FL

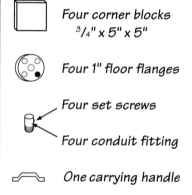

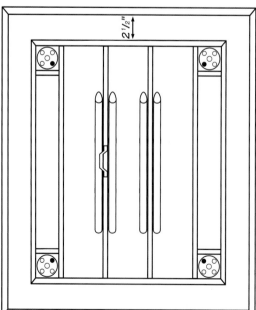

$1/2"$ quarterround molding, glue and $1^5/8"$ paneling nails

Miter all corners

Two $1/4"$ washers under front hole of 1" floor flanges

$3/4"$ #10 screws

From two 1" x 2" x 8' 1" x 2" furring on edge

Legs: Four 1" dia. conduit pipes

Four "U" clips

2 1/2"

Four corner blocks $3/4"$ x 5" x 5"

Four 1" floor flanges

Four set screws

Four conduit fitting

One carrying handle

Four 1" rubber tips

HEARTY APPLE COOKIES

1¹/₃ cup brown sugar
¹/₂ cup butter, softened
1 egg
1 cup peeled and finely chopped apple
¹/₄ cup apple juice
2 cups whole wheat flour

1 tsp. baking soda
1 tsp. cinnamon
¹/₂ tsp. salt
1 cup raisins
1 cup chopped nuts

• TOPPING •

³/₄ cup rolled oats
³/₄ cup packed brown sugar

¹/₂ tsp. cinnamon
¹/₃ cup butter, melted

Prepare topping by mixing oats, brown sugar, cinnamon and butter until crumbly. Set aside.

Beat brown sugar and butter until light and fluffy. Add egg and blend well. Beat in apple and apple juice. Lightly spoon flour into measuring cup and level off. Sift flour, baking soda, cinnamon and salt. Add to batter and mix well. Stir in raisins and nuts. Drop by heaping teaspoon about 2 inches apart on greased cookie sheet. Top each spoonful with ¹/₂ tsp. topping. Bake at 375°F for 8 to 12 minutes or until edges are golden brown. Cool for 1 minute before removing from cookie sheet.

Kevin Barnett
Troutman, NC

Index